"These stories, shared with riveting honesty, will cause you to question if you're living your Higher Purpose. And to take action to follow your heart's direction."

—ROSITA PEREZ, President, Creative Living Programs, Inc.

"Life, although sometimes seemingly desperate, through these incredible stories, raises hope, passion and proves the worth of the human spirit."

—FLORENCE SHAPIRO, Texas State Senator

"We all owe a big 'Thank You' to Jackie Waldman for introducing us to these thirty—thirty-one, counting Jackie—heroes of the spirit. Their courage, determination, and faith remind us that whatever fate comes our way, we never have to be eternal victims; we can always be triumphant survivors!"

—RABBI WAYNE DOSICK, Ph.D., author, *When Life Hurts: A Book of Hope*

"*The Courage to Give* offers readers true, inspiring stories that remind us there is always a silver lining."

—ARIELLE FORD, author of *Hot Chocolate for the Mystical Soul*

The
Courage to
Give

JACKIE WALDMAN
WITH JANIS LEIBS DWORKIS

Inspiring Stories of People Who
Triumphed Over Tragedy to Make a
Difference in the World

FOREWORD BY JOAN LUNDEN
CONCLUSION BY DANNY SIEGEL
AFTERWORD BY PATCH ADAMS

CONARI PRESS
Berkeley, California

Conari Press books are distributed by Publishers Group West.

ISBN: 1-57324-175-x

Cover and Book design: Suzanne Albertson
Cover Photography: © 1998 Michael Wilson/Image Bank
Cover Photo Handtinting: Peggy Lindt/Point Blank Design, Santa Barbara CA
Cover Art Direction: Ame Beanland

Library of Congress Cataloging-in-Publication Data

Waldman, Jackie.
    The courage to give : inspiring stories of people who triumphed over tragedy to make a difference in the world / Jackie Waldman with Janis Leibs Dworkis.
        p.   cm.
    ISBN 1-57324-175-x (trade paper)
    1. Courage Anecdotes. 2. Generosity Anecdotes. 3. Voluntarism Anecdotes. I. Dworkis. Janis Leibs. II. Title.
    BJ1533.C8W255   1999   99–16072
    179'.9–dc21s   CIP

Printed in the United States of America on recycled paper.

99 00 01 02   Data Repro   10 9 8 7 6 5 4 3 2 1

To the thirty people in this book
who recognize the potential of goodness
in all of humanity

The Courage to Give

DURING THE TWO DECADES THAT I HOSTED *Good Morning America,* I interviewed thousands of people. But I'll never forget the morning I sat across
from a woman named Virginia. Later that same morning, the man who
had brutally raped and killed her twelve-year-old daughter would be put to death.
I asked Virginia how she was dealing with her grief and the impending execution.
She began to recall the rage and anguish that had consumed her life in the years
following her daughter's murder. Unable to cope with her sorrow and anger, she
saw her marriage fall apart. Then one day as she wept to a friend she asked, "Why
is this happening to me?" Her friend replied, "A HEART FILLED WITH ANGER
HAS NO ROOM FOR LOVE!"

That was the day Virginia began to heal. She suddenly realized that although
the murderer had taken her daughter's life, Virginia's own anger and sorrow were
taking her life. Her friend told her that she needed to stop focusing on her pain
and begin to count her blessings. She couldn't change the events of the past, but
by letting go of the emotions that had paralyzed and disempowered her, she would
be free to begin living life again. No matter what our troubles are, if we can put
them aside for a moment, focus on possible solutions, and imagine a joyous
future, we can take the first step to finding peace within.

Virginia said she felt lighter as she headed home—as though a tremendous
weight had been lifted from her heart. Instead of mourning the things that were
missing in her life, she began to give thanks for her blessings—her health, her

friends, and her new understanding that our thoughts create our reality. This is a message that she felt compelled to pass on—and she began counseling others who were dealing with grief. And so, on this morning, Virginia was able to fondly remember her daughter's life, rather than dwell on her death. As for her daughter's killer, she said she was no longer holding on to any anger or hatred toward him; she felt only pity.

Those words that restored peace and instilled purpose in Virginia's life—"A HEART FILLED WITH ANGER HAS NO ROOM FOR LOVE"—have touched my life as well. I had been recently divorced and was raising three young daughters. I knew how easy it was to feel overwhelmed and alone. But that morning, I too felt a weight lift from my heart, as I decided to let go of the frustration and hurt feelings of the past and embrace the possibilities of the future. I began to write books about the power within us to heal. I found the more I give of myself through my writings, and in helping others, the more peace and fulfillment I feel in my own life. Like Virginia, I also felt the need to pass on this life-altering message—that by directing our minds, we direct our lives and ultimately create our own happiness.

When I left *Good Morning America,* I could have let my fears paralyze me again. But rather than worry about what the future would bring, and whether it would be good, I focused on what could come from this change. I now had the opportunity to take advantage of my time and to travel the country to speak about the power of our thoughts and our choices in life. This also gave me the opportunity to conquer a longtime fear of public speaking. OK, I know that millions of people saw me every morning, but I didn't see them. Speaking in person in front of even a few hundred people would unnerve me. In one of my very first speaking engagements, in Dallas, Texas, a woman named Jackie Waldman greeted me at the airport, and I was taken by her enthusiasm for life and for helping others. Later that evening, I learned that she was fighting multiple sclerosis and had gone home to rest in order to come to the evening's event. Before introducing me that night, Jackie noticed I was a bit nervous and came backstage. She told me how excited she was that I was delivering this important message about hope and the power within us to heal ourselves and to help others. Now I meet thousands of people as I travel around the country, but that night in Dallas, Jackie Waldman made me aware of the power of the message I was delivering. I was inspired by Jackie's optimism in the face of adversity, her positive approach to life and her incredible sense of purpose. She, like Virginia, exemplified the lesson that dwelling on your blessings—and reaching out to help others—helps us survive. It is easy to stay in a place of pain, wondering "Why me?" questioning life, or feeling sadness and sorrow. But if we make the effort to help someone else, we begin the healing process for ourselves.

Each one of us has the ability to answer that call to action. If we identify a need in our community or hear someone crying out for help, we can and we must answer the call. The people Jackie profiles in this book, in spite of their physical or emotional pain, heard the call and sprung into action, making a difference in our world. Their courage inspires us to remember, even in the face of adversity, our responsibility to each other and ultimately to ourselves. It's one of the most wonderful compensations of life—that no person can sincerely try to help another without helping themselves.

Susan Kandell 1999

I SEEMED TO BE LEADING A CHARMED LIFE.

At age fourteen, I had a date with a handsome guy named Steve. He took me to a Dallas Chaparrals basketball game and then to the lake where all the couples went. He took a blanket and a guitar out of the trunk of his car. And as we sat at the edge of the still water under a moonlit sky, that fifteen-year-old boy sang the most beautiful songs in the world to me, revealing his gentle soul. I knew at that moment I had met my soulmate.

Steve and I married six years later, in our senior year of college. Our parents supported us while we finished our studies, and our storybook romance continued. After college, we established ourselves in Dallas, where Steve joined his family's business. I worked as a special education teacher, but later resigned to stay at home with our three children, Melissa, Todd, and Michael. My life was filled with soccer games, gymnastics, school plays, friends, family gatherings, and the athletics that were always so important to me. I went to aerobics class every day, sometimes twice a day, and jogged three to five miles a day. In my tennis league, my nickname was "Billie Jean."

As the kids got older, I started my own business. I got the idea from a girl I met on the beach while I was in Hawaii with Steve on a business trip. She was making hair bows and taught me how to make a simple bow, too. For the rest of the vacation, she and I spent every morning on the beach in Maui making bows while our husbands were in meetings.

I bought ribbon and wire and made bows during the long flight home. When an airline attendant asked if she could buy a couple of bows for her daughter, I told her, "No way. Here, take these." She explained it was against airline regulation to accept free gifts, so we agreed on $5 per bow. My hair accessory business, Bow Jangles, was born.

And it grew. My competitive nature, which drove my love for athletics, drove me in business, too. Before long, I had twenty-five employees and twenty-five sales reps across the country. We were in every major department store and hundreds of small boutiques. During the Gulf War, we made and sold thousands of red, white, and blue bows.

I made it a point to hire Russian immigrants—teachers, scientists, engineers—

who needed to learn English before they could practice their professions in this country. We all worked together in one big room. To help them with their English, everyone spoke only English while working. But on their breaks, they were free to speak Russian. We always celebrated when one of these new Americans learned enough English to quit Bow Jangles and get back to their chosen career.

When I started my business, it was fun and more fun. But as it grew and became more successful, it also became more stressful. Before I knew it, I was getting to the office at 6:30 A.M. every morning in my attempt to run a growing business while maintaining quality family life.

It was around that time that I started having a strange tingling sensation around my waist. At first, I thought I was just imagining it. Then I attributed it to stress. Then I attributed it to some back surgery I had had years earlier.

But when the tingling progressed down my legs to my toes, and my legs became numb, I went to the doctor. After examining me, he told me to see a neurologist immediately.

The neurologist, a friend of ours, hospitalized me that day. I had MRIs of my upper and lower spine and brain. The next day, they did a spinal tap. I'll never forget lying on my stomach, with a needle in my spine, hearing one nurse whisper to another, "What are they testing for?"

The other nurse answered, "Multiple sclerosis."

I lifted my head and asked, "Is that what 'Jerry's Kids' have?"

The nurses were embarrassed that I had overheard them, and they quickly reassured me it wasn't. But, at that point I knew this was serious.

On July 12, 1991—I'll never forget that day—the doctor walked into my room and told me and Steve that I had multiple sclerosis. Even the doctor seemed sad.

He explained that nerves have a coating around them made of myelin, kind of the way telephone wires are wrapped in insulation. When telephone insulation is torn, the message we hear in the phone sounds garbled. Similarly, when myelin is torn or destroyed, messages can't flow smoothly along the nerves. And that's what my problem was. The MRI of my brain showed scars where the myelin had been destroyed. That's why my legs weren't functioning. He suggested several doctors who specialized in MS.

Steve and I held each other and cried. We were so frightened. Through my tears, I told him how sorry I was. Through his tears, he told me to quit apologizing. He told me we'd get through this together.

We chose a doctor, and he came to visit that same day. I will always remember his kind and gentle manner. After reassuring me I wasn't going to die, he told me that even though my legs were numb then, that didn't mean they would be numb forever.

He explained that MS is an autoimmune disease—meaning that the body attacks itself—that is unpredictable. Some people have an attack and return to normal. Some have an attack and are left with some damage. Others get steadily worse. Each person's MS is unique, depending on where the myelin is destroyed.

As the doctor explained it, our first priority was to halt this attack. We tried intravenous steroids first, but that didn't help. Then we tried chemotherapy. With that, some feeling returned to my legs. I was so excited. The doctor allowed me to go home and have the next two rounds of chemo at home with visiting nurses.

At home, I had to face my children, who were in middle school and high school at the time. I told each of them separately that I would not die from this and that it wasn't hereditary. I promised them nothing would change.

But of course, everything did change.

After I finished chemo and got my strength back, I assumed I would be fine. I tried to ignore the overwhelming fatigue I felt on a daily basis. I pushed myself forward, believing that if I just tried hard enough, I would beat this disease—even though I had read there was no known cure.

One day when Steve and the kids were gone, I got on the treadmill and fast-walked three miles. Sweat poured out of me triumphantly. I was so excited to be able to exercise so well again. I told myself I was feeling normal. Everything would be fine. But after I cooled down, I had to sleep for four hours.

Rabbis from our synagogue called and offered to come visit. I laughed and told them they didn't need to waste their time with me—they needed to spend time with someone who really needed them.

Looking back, I realize I was in complete denial—big time denial.

When I finally quit denying that I had a serious illness, I became very angry. Why me? Why was God punishing me? What had I done so wrong? Did I get this disease as payback for the fact that my life had gone so well? That things had come easily for me? How fair is this?

I asked these angry questions over and over and over. They went through my mind continuously. I wasn't really looking for any answers. I was just asking out of anger.

As part of my anger, I resented any happiness I saw around me. When Steve played the piano and the kids laughed and sang with him, it made me angry. When Steve came home, whistling while he cleaned the dinner dishes, and then helped the kids with homework after working all day, it made me angry. The more he did without ever complaining, the angrier I became.

How could they have fun? Didn't they know how much pain I was in? But as soon as those questions came into my mind, I would immediately feel guilty for wanting anything but happiness for the people I loved.

In 1992, because I wasn't able to work full-time anymore, I had to close my business and sell all the inventory.

I had ruined an absolutely perfect life.

Steve didn't bargain for this, I told myself over and over. Instead of wasting his time with me, he could be with an energetic, vibrant woman. Before I got sick, we loved to dance. But afterward, my legs were so weak I could barely walk without getting tired. If we did go out to a party, we never danced and we always left early. I kept thinking that he would be better off without me and that maybe I should just let him off the hook.

All day long, terrible thoughts ran through my mind. Why doesn't Steve care about the pain and turmoil I'm in? Why does he keep telling me he loves me and that my MS doesn't matter to him? What if I have to come down the aisle at my daughter's wedding in a wheelchair? What if my family is just pretending to still love me? When they were alone with their thoughts, did my children resent me?

I tried to get rid of these questions by looking everywhere for a cure for MS. I knew that cure was out there. It had to be. So I made it my full-time business to find it.

I tried Chinese herbs, acupuncture, chiropractic, and protein diets. I traveled to Israel to become part of a trial study with a new drug. I'll never forget Steve meeting the drug company representative at the airport in the middle of the night. He carried the medicine home in a special container filled with dry ice. Things looked good for a few weeks, but my body rejected the drug within a month.

Throughout everything—and no matter what I was feeling inside—I outwardly maintained a positive, cheery appearance. I made sure MS was not the focus in our home. The kids' schoolwork, outside interests, and social calendars never suffered. When friends called, I was "fine." When family called, I was "fine." If people offered help, I didn't need it.

I was even "fine" for Steve. I knew he felt my pain and devastation. But I couldn't bring myself to talk openly about my feelings with him. I didn't want to feel his pain. I just couldn't face it. I had enough of my own.

I did have one dear friend, Dee, who understood me almost better than I understood myself. She had two rocking chairs on her front porch, and we spent many, many hours just rocking and talking. I often thought how good it was those chairs couldn't talk—they knew way too much.

Dee never sympathized with me. She never judged my anger. Instead, she talked about Eastern religion and philosophy. And she talked about the book *A Course in Miracles*.

Many days Dee made me angry with her calm, peaceful manner. I was frustrated by her daily affirmations, her quest for inner peace, her belief in God as an encompassing Source of unconditional love within each of us. I told her the philosophy was easy for her to embrace—but just wait until she suffered in some way. And that's when she told me about her childhood, about growing up with an alcoholic single mom, about being on her own by the time she was seventeen, about having faith and choosing love.

I'd leave Dee's house thinking about how impressed I was with her courage. It didn't occur to me to think about how I could apply her philosophy to my life.

When the movie *Schindler's List* came out, Dee and I went to see it. After the movie, we rocked on her porch and talked about how one person's kind act could make such a difference. By not giving in to the Nazis, Oskar Schindler saved 1,000 lives and, indirectly, all the future generations that would be born to those people.

As Dee and I talked about the power of Schindler's kind acts, we began to brainstorm the idea of a week in Dallas celebrating the value of kindness as part of the National Random Acts of Kindness™ Month. And we decided to turn those ideas into reality. We asked Jim McCormick, a well-respected businessman in Dallas, to be the chair.

The week of February 7–14, 1995 was a miracle. Rosa Parks, Martin Luther King III, W. Deen Mohammed, and Dennis Weaver came to Dallas and spoke at kindness rallies, at schools, and at interfaith services. Under the guidance of

Police Chief Ben Click, the Dallas Police Department handed out "kindness citations" that week.

We had a kindness rally for 10,000 school children. Girls from the YWCA handed out hot chocolate to downtown workers as they left their buildings; kids with learning differences made art exhibits depicting kindness; a kindness song, "We Believe," was written; 800 Christian, Jewish, and Muslim children heard a Sunday School lesson taught together by Martin Luther King III and Dennis Weaver; children and adult choirs sang in malls; the African American Museum held a reception in honor of kindness; and Lovers Lane United Methodist Church hosted a fifty-year celebration of the liberation of the Nazi war camps.

Kindness was everywhere in the media—radio talk shows, television morning shows, the news, even on the front page of the *Dallas Morning News*. Billboards proclaiming kindness were everywhere.

And throughout all the planning and all the activities, Dee kept reminding me to watch the miracles, to see the love, to see God. And as tired as I was, I *did* feel a new energy. That's what kept me going.

When Kindness Week was over, I didn't want those good feelings to end. Since I wasn't working or doing athletics, I thought I might spend some time volunteering. So I called the Dallas Memorial Center for Holocaust Studies and trained to become a docent.

Soon I was speaking to fifty middle school children each week when I took them on tours of the center. We stood in a boxcar—a real boxcar that had been used to transport Jews to the Nazi death camps, that had been donated to our museum—and I told them, "When you leave here, do not hate Nazis. Vow in your own heart never to be prejudiced. That's how you can make a difference."

During each tour, when I told them about a particular survivor who lost his parents and brothers and sister, I always started to cry—it was the man who had founded this center so that could never happen again. I left the tour each week exhausted—but feeling new energy that I had discovered. And kids wrote me letters affirming that same feeling of hope and love.

For the very first time since my MS diagnosis, I was feeling someone else's pain and not thinking about myself.

I liked the way I was feeling. And so I took on more volunteer jobs. Within a year, I was serving on the boards of several schools, as co-vice president of community service of the National Council of Jewish Women, as our neighborhood March of Dimes volunteer—and the list goes on. I said Yes to everyone.

Right around that time, I happened into a used bookstore. An old copy of Wayne Dyer's book, *Real Magic*, caught my eye. I had never heard of Wayne Dyer, but the picture of the rainbow on the cover and the subtitle *Creating Miracles in Everyday Life* attracted me to the book. I grabbed it, paid for it, and went home.

I could not believe what I was reading. Everything I had been feeling since Kindness Week was written in this book. Dyer wrote of creating real magic in your life, which he describes as those times when we can see beyond the concrete five senses and know there is more. He wrote of going within and discovering that our purpose in life is to love unconditionally and to live a life of service. He spoke about life not being a "What's in it for me" experience, but being about our spiritual selves having a human experience.

He asked the reader to have an open mind when first learning about spirituality and to suspend disbelief. Then he talked about intuition, the divine spark within each of us that we can access whenever we choose. He suggested that readers go within and be quiet, to listen to the voice within. And he spoke about waking each day and being grateful for the smallest of things, to enjoy the journey instead of working only for an outcome. If we can do these things, miracles begin to occur.

I can only describe my experience of reading that book as an instant awakening. In one moment, every piece of my life became crystal clear. I knew that I had lived my life not seeing "real" magic. In that one moment, I knew without a doubt exactly who I was—not a person with a disease and weak legs, but a person who has a heart filled with love and wants to be of service.

I felt a lightness I had not felt in years. And my healing began.

At that point, I understood that my healing isn't about searching for the cure to multiple sclerosis. There is no cure for MS. My healing is about healing *within*. It's about being motivated by ethics, serenity, and quality of life—not achievement, performance, and acquisitions.

And I suddenly knew loving guidance was always available to me. All I had to do was ask. I have never felt alone again. I knew my purpose was to serve others—that's why my service work always gave me new energy.

About a year later, I said, "God, OK, I'm really stretched. I keep saying 'Yes' to everyone. I promise I'll say 'Yes' to whatever YOU ask me to do. What's next?"

Less than a week later, I woke up and looked at Steve. "OK, I got my marching orders. I'm writing a book, and I've been told exactly what it is about. It's about people who have suffered physical or emotional pain, and gone beyond their own pain to help someone else. I need to interview them and write their stories."

From February through May I did preliminary research. I sent a short proposal to Danny Siegel, author, poet, and the king of finding community service heroes. He called me and told me he would help me. God bless Danny Siegel. He told me about Bea Salazar. I interviewed Bea and wrote and rewrote her story. In July I knew I needed a professional writer to make this work.

It had always been a dream of mine to write a book, but I decided this idea was too righteous to waste time on learning how to write. I thought about calling Janis Dworkis, an acquaintance and local writer, but I really was not sure. Then one day

I opened the phone book, and the header on the right-hand page said "Dworkis." I smiled and immediately called her.

Janis came on board July 20, the day before my birthday. I never liked celebrating my birthday. But, this year I had reason to celebrate. I was living with purpose.

I interviewed Jonni McCuin and Ben Beltzer. We wrote their stories and finished the proposal. We mailed it to three publishers in October. Three weeks later Mary Jane Ryan called from Conari Press. She told me they wanted to publish our book.

After crying—and trying to sound somewhat coherent—I hung up the phone and sat very still. I thanked God for the miracle, for giving me this incredible gift to share with the world. I laughed at the synchronicity—of course the publisher would be the same group that published all of the Random Acts of Kindness[TM] books.

From October to December I interviewed all thirty people, and Janis and I wrote their stories. Each day, as I spoke with the folks we profiled here, I learned a new lesson. Their strength, kindness, and inspiration fed my soul. They gave me the energy to finish an entire manuscript within weeks.

Meeting thirty new friends who have endured incredible pain, yet are reaching out and helping so many others, reminds me daily of the miracles of life.

Recently I found a newspaper clipping featuring me as a child with two other children. It was in the *Dallas Times Herald,* in 1956. I was four years old. The caption reads, "Socks Away—three tiny members of Temple Emanu-El sort through 563 pairs of socks they and fellow church school members have collected for the City-County Department of Public Welfare to give needy youngsters at Christmas. The children gave socks to the program in place of exchanging Chanukah gifts among themselves."

I cried looking at the joy and love in my little face. At four years old, I had known the peace and joy of service to others. But for so many years, I had forgotten the truth of that little girl. I cried tears of gratitude for the gift of remembering who I really am.

I cried for the miracle of life, for the chance I and we all have been given to offer our unique gifts to the world, gifts born, so often, from our very woundedness.

So now, I invite you to meet my thirty new friends. These are special people—all of whom continue to teach me a lesson I had once known long ago, but had forgotten. These wonderful people have the courage we all need, the courage to see beyond. The admiration and love I feel in my heart for each of them will stay with me always. Their stories have changed me, as I hope they will change you.

I thank God for showing me the way. And I thank these people for revealing their stories to all of us.

CHAPTER 1

Susan Kandell 1999

Be Happy, Be Useful

BEA SALAZAR

THERE WAS A TIME IN MY LIFE when I was in so much physical and emotional pain that I just didn't think I could go on. I spent every day and every night thinking about my pain and how useless my life had become.

Then one morning, I found a little boy in a Dumpster. And the minute I saw him, I realized that there were children whose pain was much greater than my own. God led me to find that child, and to find all the children I've worked with since that day. In working to help those children, my own pain has been diminished. And my life has become a tremendous joy. —————————————————————

Until 1986, I was "Super Mom." I was a single mother of five children—my husband left us when my youngest was two years old—and I worked very hard to do everything I could for them. My three boys were in high school playing football that year, and my two girls were on the drill team. Life wasn't easy, but my children were doing well, and I was paying the bills. So I considered myself lucky.

I worked the night shift in a factory during those years. I got off work at 7 A.M., and I'd try to get home as fast as I could to see the kids as they were leaving for school. I was so tired that I usually left work with my eyes half-closed. I would undo my bra and take off my shoes in the car. After I said good-bye to the kids, I would nap until three o'clock.

After school, I would pick up the kids, make dinner, feed everyone, and make sure they did their homework. And then I went back to work at 11 P.M.

One day, all that fatigue caught up with me—and my life changed forever. I stood up on a stool at work to change a part in one of the huge machines. But my foot slipped, the stool gave way, and I fell right into the machine. I felt a shooting pain from my groin up to my eyes. Then everything just went black. When I woke up, I couldn't put my legs together. Blood was everywhere. I was taken to the hospital in an ambulance.

The doctors told me I had a separated pelvis and two slipped discs. All I knew was that I was in such horrible pain—suffering that I don't wish on anybody. I had surgery that was supposed to help. But it didn't seem to do much good. I was in constant, terrible agony.

After the accident, I tried to go back to work because we needed the money so badly, but the pain was too severe. I was supposed to get money from the factory's insurance company, but that was tied up for a long time. We almost lost our apartment and our car. My children wanted to drop out of school and go to work to pay rent. But I said no. I had worked so hard to take care of them, and they were all doing so well. I would not let them drop out of school to do the job I was supposed to be doing.

Before too long, I became very depressed. I had no money. I was in constant pain. I was a mother who couldn't even take care of her children any longer. I felt like I was good for nothing.

I started having thoughts of suicide.

Those thoughts scared me, because I knew my children still needed me. So I called a social service agency in Carrollton, Texas, where I lived, and I spoke to a wonderful lady named Anna. She counseled me, and the agency paid our rent and gave us groceries.

Anna was a tremendous help to me and to my whole family. But my pain just didn't seem to get better. One day, when the kids were at school, I sat in my bedroom with the door closed and looked at a bottle of my pain pills.

"What if I took all these pills at one time?" I thought.

At that moment, it didn't seem like such a bad idea. Then I started to cry, thinking about my children and the fact that I just didn't want to suffer anymore. Right then I heard someone knocking at my door. The knocking kept going on and on. Finally I had to get up to answer the door.

There was Anna. I started to cry. God had sent her to me. She had saved my life.

Anna checked on me three times a day after that. She made sure I showed up for counseling. She really helped me. After a while, I began to handle my pain better, and I began to feel better mentally, too. Even after Anna stopped coming to see me because she had taken another job out of town, I could tell I was getting better. I started to think that maybe I did have a future. I still wasn't able to go back to work, but I was able to do more and more for myself and my children, and more chores around the house.

It was one of those chores that changed the course of my life.

I had gone outside to throw the trash away, and I heard something moving in the Dumpster. When I peered over the edge, I saw a little boy from a nearby apartment in there. He was digging around in that garbage looking for something to eat. I had never seen anything like that in my life.

I got him out of the Dumpster and took the piece of dirty bread he had found out of his hand and threw it away. Then he started to cry, and I realized he wanted that bread because he was hungry. So I took him into my apartment and I made him a peanut butter and jelly sandwich. Then I sent him home.

I was still thinking about that poor little boy about fifteen minutes later when someone knocked on my door. When I went to open it, I saw six five-year-olds standing there.

"Is it true you're giving peanut butter sandwiches away?" one of the little boys asked me.

"No, I'm not," I said. "But if you're hungry, come on in. I'll feed you."

So I fixed them all peanut butter and jelly sandwiches and I sent them all home. The next day I had thirteen hungry kids at my door. And I made some more sandwiches.

Then I started asking some questions. I asked people why there were so many hungry children in our neighborhood. And they explained that these children got free lunches at school. But this was June and school was out, and so they didn't have anyone to give them lunch. Their parents worked, and they had to wait until their parents came back at night to eat.

I couldn't imagine it. I had worked so hard to provide for my own kids. And I was still trying hard to provide—by this time I was on disability insurance. I realized that I had been so busy taking care of my own five children that I hadn't noticed the needs of the other children right around me.

I picked up the phone. I called the social service agency where Anna had worked. And then I called my church. I told everyone what was happening to these children. I told them I wanted to help, but I couldn't do it alone.

Did I ever get help! I had so much peanut butter and jelly and bread delivered to my apartment that I still have a jar of peanut butter from that first donation—and that was eight years ago. With that food, I made some sandwiches and I made some Kool Aid and I started feeding the neighborhood children from out of my apartment.

We had so much fun that summer. We watched movies, we talked about God, we played games. I tried to teach them about cleanliness. A lot of the children had head lice, so I tried to clean their hair and get rid of the lice.

The kids came every day the whole summer, and we spent all day doing things together. I just fell in love with these children. They were so nice, but so poor. And they were just completely unattended. No one was taking care of them.

At the end of the summer, when it was time for school to start, the kids were sad. And so was I. Helping these kids had given me a reason to live.

My apartment felt so empty and quiet that first day of school—much too quiet. But that afternoon, there was a knock on the door. And when I opened it, a few of the kids were standing there.

"Bea, we need help with our schoolwork," they said. "Will you help us with math? With you help us with reading?"

"Of course I will," I told them, my eyes filled with tears. "Come on in." I was just so glad they were back.

I believe God called me to do this work. God needed someone to look after these kids—and that someone was me. When God calls you to do something, you don't fight that. You go with it.

So in 1990, I formally established a nonprofit organization called Bea's Kids. I went to the management of my building to ask for help, and they gave me an empty one-bedroom apartment where I could take care of thirty kids after school. Within one month, I had sixty kids. So the management gave me a two-bedroom apartment. And that's where my volunteers and I have been taking caring of our children for the past eight years.

Our whole community is involved now. We have volunteers help us from local schools and businesses. People in the community donate thousands of dollars worth of used items, and we sell them once a year in a gigantic garage sale. We use the money to buy school supplies, shoes, socks, and underwear. Twice a year, at Christmas and when school starts, we buy everyone new shoes. Eight years ago, these children didn't have socks and underwear. But now they don't have to worry about that. They didn't have pens or pencils or paper—but now they do. Someone even donated a computer for them to use.

I feel like these children are all my own. And I'm so proud of them. They are doing so well. These children know what is expected of them when they come into our program, and they know how important they are to us. Our kids are not on drugs. And our girls are not pregnant. They have a clear direction in life. I even have a group of kids graduating from high school this year, kids who have been with me for eight years. Some of them are even going on to college.

I am so blessed. These children are the reason I'm here now. That's why I'm living—to help them. Even when I have days when I can barely walk because of my injuries, I get up and get going because I know my kids need me. They give me a purpose. In fact, they've given me much more than I've ever given them.

I know now that this is why God saved my life. This is why he sent Anna to knock on my door that day just when I was thinking about swallowing a whole bottle of pills. He saved my life because He needs me to take care of these children.

There are so many children who need help everywhere. And there are people in apartment complexes everywhere who could help. I tell people, Open your doors, open your hearts. Help a child with their math homework. Help them with their reading. Just love them. No one is tending to the children any more. And we need to. They need us.

I've learned a wonderful lesson from these kids—a lesson I will never forget. I've learned that the only truly happy people are those who have found a way to be useful.

Join Bea in her effort to make today's children tomorrow's leaders. Contact: Bea's Kids, 1517 Metrocrest #129, Carrollton, Texas 75006. Tel: 971-417-9061. Web site: **www.princeofpeace.org/beaskids.htm**. In Canada, contact the United Way of Regina, 2022 Halifax Street, Regina, SK S4P 1T7. Tel: 306-757-5671.

CHAPTER 2

Susan Kandell 1999

Faith Kaplan and Jim Kane

David's Legacy

FAITH KAPLAN

O N NOVEMBER 14, 1992, my sixteen-year-old son, David, was with his friends at a school dance. I went to a movie with my twelve-year-old daughter Kristy and one of her friends. We asked David to come with us, but he said the dance sounded like more fun. And I really couldn't blame him. Later that night, he called home to ask if he could spend the night at his friend's house after the dance. My husband, Steve, and I said sure.

We didn't know David would never come home again.

Kristy and I just couldn't fall asleep that night. We kept tossing and turning, dozing for a minute and then waking up. Then all of a sudden, I saw an enormous, bright white light in front of my face, and I sat up in bed and yelled, "David!"

I had no idea what was happening at the time. I didn't know what I was seeing, or why I was screaming out David's name. I thought it was just a bad dream. But ten minutes after that bright light woke me, the police called to say David had been in a car accident.

The light I had seen was the light David saw as a car came directly toward him. I truly believe that. That's how strong the bond is between a mother and child.

When we got to the hospital, the police told us what had happened. David and his friend had gone for a walk. They were trying to cross a busy street in the pitch dark. David accidentally stepped off the curb directly into the path of an oncoming car. There was no way for the driver to avoid him.

We were allowed to see David for just one brief minute, and then they took him by helicopter to a nearby major medical center. It took us thirty minutes to drive there—probably the longest thirty minutes of my life.

When we got there, two doctors met us and started discussing David's injuries. They told us he might lose his leg, and I was OK with that. They told us he might have some brain damage, and I was OK with that, too. I just wanted him to live. But then they started talking about how his brain was swelling and there was a chance he wasn't going to make it.

And that's when they asked us if we would consider organ donation.

"Yes," we said.

That was our answer, our total answer. We didn't need any time to ask questions or discuss any issues because we had already discussed it as a family a few months earlier. We had been aware of the need for organ donors because Kristy has diabetes. And although she wasn't in need of a transplant herself, we decided as a family that we would donate our organs if the need arose.

At the time of that discussion, of course, we all thought we were talking about the possibility of Steve or I becoming a donor. Never the children.

We only had David with us for two days after that. We sat with him while we waited for the swelling to go down, while we waited for him to show signs of life. But over those two days, his body just shut down. We had already signed the necessary papers, so when his brain was no longer alive, the doctors harvested every single part of him that anyone could possibly use. That's what we told them to do.

Initially, the fact that we had donated David's organs was of no comfort to us whatsoever. All we knew was that we had lost our David—our Deedle, our D. J.— one of the sweetest souls to ever hit this earth. We cried and we screamed, then we cried and screamed some more. Nothing we did, and nothing we thought, could help us make sense of such a tragedy.

David was such a special boy. Everyone loved him. He was the kind of guy who was always going out of his way to help other people. If there was an activity at school, David was the one who volunteered to help clean up afterward. If the neighbors' lawns needing mowing, David was the one who showed up to do it— at no charge. If a friend needed him, he was there.

David loved music and swimming and laughing and movies and fishing and taking long walks in the woods. But I think his two favorite loves were cooking and The Three Stooges. That boy could just cook up a storm. He had a natural talent for it. He loved to see the pleasure on people's faces as they tasted the foods he had prepared. And he also loved to laugh. Maybe his laugh is what we missed the most.

About a month after his death, we received a letter from the New England Organ Bank. They gave us some general information about the people who had received David's organs. His corneas, kidneys, liver, pancreas, and heart had all been transplanted. I was mostly intrigued about his heart. We were told the recipient was a forty-one-year-old retired police officer with two sons, ages eleven and thirteen. We knew that whoever got David's heart would be especially lucky, because this was a boy with a wonderful heart.

We went through the next many months just going through the motions. We had good days and bad days, but mostly bad. I broke my back in a fall and missed a lot of work. Eventually, I was laid off. At my doctor's suggestion, I started exercising again, which I had not been doing since David's death. I started going to the gym a few times a week and I kept it up.

About two years later, Steve and I got a letter from David's heart recipient, sent to us through the organ bank. He had written to thank us. He could only tell us his first name, Jim, because organ banks have rules about protecting privacy. And we wrote him back, through the organ bank, telling him about ourselves and David, and how much his note meant to us. After corresponding like that for a while, we decided we wanted to meet. The organ bank said they would check on the protocol about that and get back to us.

I was so excited about the possibility of meeting Jim—nervous, but excited. One night, on the way out of the health club, I stopped to talk to the owner, Paul, about it.

"Guess what, Paul—I think I'm going to get to meet my son's heart recipient," I told him. "This man—his name is Jim—has been writing to us, and I think the organ bank is going to arrange a meeting."

"Did you say his name is Jim?" Paul asked incredulously.

"Yes."

"Oh, my God. Faith, you already know this man. You work out with his wife all the time. And Jim comes here, too."

At first I didn't believe him. I couldn't. But Paul told me that a woman who worked out there had been telling him how her husband, Jim, was going to be meeting his donor's family. Right that minute, Paul called Jim on the phone and asked him the name of his donor's mother.

"Faith?" he repeated. "Jim, she's standing right in front of me right this minute. I think you need to get down here."

My whole body turned to jelly. I was pacing and shaking, and people were standing around crying. Then all of a sudden, a man came through the door and Paul said, "That's him."

I walked right up to Jim and just looked at him. And then I said, "I want to give you a hug." I felt like I was thanking him for keeping a part of David alive. And I gave him a picture of David.

We had always been glad that we had donated David's organs, but the full meaning of the gift hadn't hit me until that minute. Here was a man who never thought he would live to see his sons in high school, but he has. He had been on the waiting list for a heart for two years, because of viral damage to his heart. And before David died, Jim had been hospitalized for forty-eight days, not knowing whether he would live long enough to receive a new heart. Now he's an active dad and husband, looking forward to grandchildren one day.

Meeting Jim Kane gave me back my life.

Seeing his happiness and how much his family loved him snapped me out of the depression I had been in since David's death. When David first died, I really lost all faith in God and everything else. I was just so angry—at life, at God, at every single thing I could think of. I was just a shell of a person.

But Jim completely turned my life around. I knew I had to dedicate myself to promoting organ donation from that moment forward. No one knows more than I do how hard it can be for the donor family. But meeting Jim, I also fully understood what a true gift of life it is.

Once I met Jim and became active in promoting organ donation, I was able to begin my own healing process. It soothed me to know that I was really helping other people. Organ donation is such an emotionally difficult topic, and that's why doctors avoid it so often. They wait and wait to find the right time to talk to the family about it. But that perfect moment rarely comes. You just have to step up and ask anyway—so others can live.

I also started visiting families who had lost teens. I don't even know how that started. But when I would read in the paper about a teen who had died, I knew I had to see that family. I would just pick up the phone and introduce myself. I wanted to be with them. No one could understand their pain better than someone who had been through it. I just want to bring them whatever comfort I possibly could.

Since we met, Jim and I have participated in many public events together. We've spoken at meetings and seminars. We walked a Toys for Tots road race together. I've handed out donor cards at several Boston Marathons and worked for the National Kidney Foundation for several years now, including their motorcycle run.

Last year, we got very involved with a little girl in our community of Attleboro, Massachusetts, who needed a liver transplant. We had read about her story in the paper, and called the family to say we were there to help. We volunteered for everything—blood drives, fund-raising, giving out organ donor cards. When she finally got her liver, I went to the hospital and spent the night with the family. And the little girl did just great.

Our story—actually, the story of David and Jim—has received a lot of publicity. And we think that's great. Because every time someone hears about us, we know that one more family is considering organ donation. And one more family waiting in a hospital room has been given new hope.

So every time I see someone sign a donor card, I give thanks.

"David," I say, "look what you've done. This is your legacy."

There are many ways you can give the gift of life. Find out how to become involved. Contact: The National Kidney Foundation, 30 East 33rd Street, New York, New York 10016. Tel: 800-622-9010. In Canada, contact The Kidney Foundation of Canada National Office, 300-5165 Sherbrooke Street West, Montreal, QC H4A 1T6. E-mail: webmaster@kidney.ca.

CHAPTER 3

Andy Shivers 1999

A Solid Foundation

MILLARD FULLER

M Y MOTHER DIED WHEN I WAS THREE YEARS OLD, and a few years later my father married the church organist. So from the time I was very young, church was a big part of our lives. We had church and Sunday school on Sunday mornings, prayer service on Wednesday nights, and revivals every fall.

Our church took care of its own—but only its own. If a member became sick, the preacher and other church members went to see them and always brought flowers. It was a loving and caring fellowship, and that's not bad. But we never reached a hand out farther than our own little circle. There was, of course, support for foreign missionary work, but little outreach locally.

I can tell you now for sure, that hand never reached out far enough. ───────────────────────────

My family always played an active role in our church and we were serious about wanting to follow God. But my father emphasized that financial success in the eyes of the world was always important, too. So I knew, growing up, that I wanted to make a big pile of money one day. I decided I could get rich and also be faithful. From elementary school through law school, I always had a money-making project going on the side.

Since I had lost my mother at such a young age, I always dreamed about the type of loving family I would have when I grew up. I married my wife, Linda, when I was twenty-four years old. She was only eighteen at the time. I loved her dearly, but the truth is that as time went along, I became more devoted to making money than to her.

With a partner from law school, I opened a law office in Montgomery, Alabama. Through that business partnership, we made money in just about everything we tried. We sold tractor cushions, we published cookbooks, we sold candy. Everything we did turned into money.

I bought a beautiful house for Linda and hired a maid to help her with the housework and our two children. I made sure she drove a Lincoln Continental. My partner and I bought 2,000 acres of land. We bought cattle and horses. We had a fishing lake, a lake house, and speedboats. And we still attended church pretty regularly. I had set my goals and surpassed them. I was feeling good about my life.

When, in 1964, the company treasurer walked into my office and announced that I was worth a million dollars, I wasn't even surprised.

"What's your next goal?" she asked me.

"Ten million," I answered without hesitation. "Why not?"

But not too long after that, Linda walked into my office and told me something that changed my life forever.

"Millard, I don't love you anymore," she said through her tears. "You are married to your business. I loved you at one time, but I don't even know who you are any more. I can't stay in this loveless marriage."

I was so stunned, so shocked, that I don't even remember what I said. Every single thing I had ever been involved with in my life up to that point had been a success. Success was all I knew. It had never even occurred to me that my marriage wouldn't be a success, too.

From where I stood, I had a wonderful wife whom I loved dearly, lovely children, a beautiful home, a successful business. Everything was great. But from where Linda stood, she saw an empty life. And she was a smart lady. She knew the difference between a house filled with things and a home filled with love.

I promised her things would change. But they didn't. A year later, Linda left me and went to New York to seek counseling from a pastor she knew. I felt helpless and, for the first time in my life, totally out of control. I had no idea what to do. I was terrified that I might lose her. So I followed her to New York.

When I saw Linda in New York—and saw the sadness and despair all over her face—it just broke my heart. I resolved to do whatever it took to keep our family together.

Right there on Fifth Avenue, we took each other in our arms and cried. "Linda, I never wanted to make you unhappy. I love you so much," I told her that day. "I never meant to turn away from your love."

We hailed a cab and told each other all the ways we had each backed away from each other and the Lord and focused our attention on other things. "Linda, I know what we should do," I said, and I looked at her. "I think we need to give away all our money. We need to give it away and make ourselves available for whatever God wants us to do." And she agreed.

The very first thing we did was to go home, pick up our kids, and spend some time together as a family. We drove through Georgia and Florida, just taking the time to get to know each other again. On a whim, we drove to Americus, Georgia, to spend a few hours at a place I'd heard about called Koinonia Farm. I had a friend at the farm, and he introduced me to Clarence Jordan. We ended up staying a month.

Clarence was a radical Christian, and he thought our idea to give our money away made perfect sense. In the middle of the South, Clarence and his wife Florence had founded Koinonia as an integrated community for people to live together and support themselves in harmony. Clarence was way ahead of his time. The love we felt at Koinonia and the beauty of our acceptance there was something we never forgot.

Then we went home and made the necessary arrangements to give away our money. We made sure it would go to people who truly needed it. With every dollar we gave to help someone else, the better we started to feel. As we unburdened ourselves from the weight of our worldly possessions, we waited to see what God wanted us to do.

Two years later, after working with a church-related college, we returned to Koinonia Farm. There, with Clarence Jordan, I organized a housing program called "Partnership Housing" for local poor families. The homes these families were living in were little more than shacks, if that. Most had no plumbing or insulation, and the electricity consisted of one light bulb hanging from an exposed wire. The roofs did little to keep out leaves, much less water. These landless families had no hope to afford anything better. But we wanted to give them that hope.

The first house we worked on was for Bo and Emma Johnson. Sadly, Clarence died of a heart attack before that house was completed. But Linda and I were committed to finishing the work. And when we did finish, the Johnsons had a solid, concrete-block house with a modern kitchen, an indoor bathroom, and a good heating system. Their monthly mortgage on a twenty-year loan was $25. They cried. We all cried for the joy and love we all felt.

For five years, we built houses for people, and we clearly saw the difference decent housing made in people's lives. Then, for three years, we built houses in Africa. In 1976, we returned to Americus; it was then that we founded Habitat for Humanity.

Habitat is based on the guiding principle that all people deserve a decent place to live. And with enough people working together across this planet, I am convinced that we can abolish poverty housing altogether. So far, Habitat has provided housing for more than 350,000 people in more than 1,500 U.S. cities and sixty other countries. In 1998, we dedicated our 70,000th house.

Habitat doesn't work in a vacuum. The homeowners-to-be work directly with us to build their homes. And during that time, wonderful relationships are forged. But the most wonderful times of all are the dedication ceremonies, when the homeowners receive the keys to their new house and a Bible. Not much in my life touches me more than that. Every time, it's just one big love fest when the homeowners realize how many people really do care about them and are willing to turn that love into action.

I remember one homeowner in Wisconsin. She wanted to speak to the volunteers when she received her keys and Bible, but she couldn't say a word. She just cried and cried. She had asked her neighbors to come over so she could show them her beautiful new house, and they were so excited.

"Look at this beautiful bathroom. Oh, look at these cabinets—and this door." You could hear the excitement in the neighbors' voices as they filed through the house. But the woman couldn't answer them.

You just can't underestimate the impact that a safe, decent house can make on a family's life. I met one young boy who told me that his new home changed his outlook on school.

"I used to be bad in school. The teacher thought I was a bad person. But I was just worried we would have to move back into our car. Now, I get Bs all the time," he said proudly.

As she shook my hand, one mother told me her new home improved her son's health. "Timmy used to have asthma all the time. But now our house is warm and safe, and he's off all medication," she said with tears in her eyes. "He feels great."

A solid home can absolutely transform a child's life, but Habitat's homes transform the volunteers, too. How can you not feel the love that comes from dozens of people working side by side for days at a time toward a common, worthwhile goal? Yes, we get sweaty and caked with dirt and paint, and more tired than we thought was possible. But we're doing the work the Lord told us to do—we are taking care of His people. What could possibly feel better?

I doubt anyone has felt Habitat's power to transform lives more than I have. I was on the verge of losing everything that truly meant anything to me. I had gone so far down the wrong track that I hadn't even noticed how empty my life had become. But when I turned my attention to helping other people, I healed myself and I healed my relationships with the people I loved.

In some ways, I'm the same person I was all those years ago. I'm still a hard worker, and I still want to succeed at what I'm doing. I'm still at the office at 5 A.M. sometimes. I'm still in meetings all day long some days.

What's different is that my goals have changed. Now I'm focused on building the Kingdom of God on earth. And my little part of that is to build houses for the poor.

You can profess to be religious from today until tomorrow, but if you don't back up those beliefs with appropriate action, then they're like cotton candy—they look good, but there's nothing to sink your teeth into. I lived a life of cotton candy for years. I thank God that He opened up my eyes in time for me to make more of a difference with my life than that.

Join in making simple, decent, and affordable housing a reality for those in need. Contact: Habitat for Humanity International, 121 Habitat Street, Americus, Georgia 31709-3498. Tel: 912-924-6935. Web site: **www.habitat.org.**

Susan Kandell 1999

Breaking Free

DONNA KLAFFKE

PRISONS COME IN ALL SHAPES AND SIZES. Some are rooms with locked doors. Others are the prisons of ignorance created by a lack of education.

I have lived in both of those prisons. I know what it means to be locked in a room for months at a time. And I know what it means to lack the skills you need to reach even your most basic goals. That's why I am on a mission to help as many people as possible get those skills. That's why I'm still working on them myself. _____

I grew up in an environment that was so abusive, it's sometimes hard for people to believe my story. My parents divorced when I was a toddler, and my two older sisters and I were given to my father to raise. He remarried a woman who had two children of her own, and then they had another child together. So there were six children in the house all together.

From the time my biological parents divorced until I was about eight years old, I spent my life locked in a room with no food and no toilet. When I was allowed out, I would have to stand for hours in a corner on my tiptoes with my chin up on the wall and my hands behind my back. My biological sisters were beaten and abused, too, although they were not locked up.

Sometimes I would go for days without getting anything to eat. My sisters would try to sneak something in to me to eat, but if they got caught they were beaten for trying to help me. That was the worst. Hearing my sisters screaming while they were being beaten and not being able to do anything about it—that was worse than anything else that happened to me.

Every now and then, I would be allowed to go to school for a short while. When I did go, my total concentration was on how to steal someone's lunch. No child who is abused comes to school to think about math or English. I came to school to get away from the beatings for a little while, and to get some food. Of course, I would get caught stealing, and that would get me in trouble. Then I would be forced to stay home some more.

So I didn't really learn anything during those years. I didn't learn reading or writing or math. I didn't even learn the basics of how to interact with other people in a normal way. I didn't have the chance.

I'm not sure how I made it through those years. But I know I had a very strong spirit. I believed in my heart that somewhere there was someone who loved me. And I knew that I had not been born just to be beaten all the time.

I was finally removed from that house when I was about eight. I don't really remember how it happened. Maybe someone in the government finally found out what was going on. But after that, I became a ward of the state. For the next eight years or so, I went from one foster home to the next, many of them as abusive in their own way as my father's home had been.

I did go to school for a little while during middle school and high school. But every time, just when I was starting to feel safe enough to relax and be able to learn something, I was moved to a new place. Sometimes I would just be lost in the system and wouldn't go to school at all.

I taught myself to read during those years. I did it by picking up anything that looked like it would interest me. I remember reading love stories in magazines. I didn't really understand the words at first. But I would just keep reading and reading and after awhile, I would start to recognize some of the words. Eventually, I could read just about anything. I always wanted to learn writing and spelling. But I never did. I did teach myself how to add and subtract, though. But I never learned my times tables and never completed high school.

At the last hearing I remember, I took my biological mother to court because she was trying to turn me into a prostitute. I refused to do that, no matter what. The judge told me that after all I had been through—after all the places I had lived and all the injustices that happened to me—that if I could prove that I could live on my own, get a job and a place to live, I could be my own guardian.

And that's what I did. Finally, I had my freedom. Finally.

I don't know exactly how old I was when that happened. I know I didn't have a driver's license yet. But my age during those years was always kind of a blur. I didn't live anyplace that had birthdays or Christmases or any other way to mark the years. So there was nothing for me ever to judge one year from another. I think I was about fifteen or sixteen. But I'm not sure.

When I was about seventeen, I got into a bad marriage. The man had money, and I thought being with him was a good idea. But he became abusive, so I got right out of there. I walked away with nothing but the clothes on my back. But I didn't care. I wasn't going to stay in an abusive situation ever again.

After that, I got jobs washing dishes, cleaning houses, anything I could do to feed myself. To someone else, it might not sound very appealing to be riding a bicycle home from work at midnight. But to me, it was freedom. I never got on welfare. I never turned to drugs. And I wasn't living with anyone who was hurting me. That was worth just about everything to me.

When I was about twenty, I realized I needed help. That early marriage was a sign to me that I was in danger of perpetuating this pattern of abuse for my whole life. I didn't want to do that. I didn't want to get married again and abuse my own children just because I didn't know any other way to be. I knew I had to learn to love myself and believe that I was worthwhile. But I didn't know how to do that on my own.

So one day, I just walked into the mental health services office in my hometown and asked for help. I told them about my background and told them I didn't have any money. And they directed me to Dr. Silvers. It took me a long time to open up to him. But once I could trust him, I found that he and I worked well together. And he helped me so much.

I waited five years before I would even consider getting married again. And I did remarry when I was in my twenties. My husband is an architect, and I have two wonderful boys who are now eleven and fourteen. I own my own cleaning business, but I spend as much time with my children as I possibly can.

I was honest with my husband from the beginning about my background and about what I could and could not do. He knew I could read. But he also knew I wanted to learn how to write and spell. I tried to get help for a while, but it never worked out.

Then one day, my husband brought me a flier from Literacy Volunteers of America (LVA). I let the phone number sit there for about a year. Finally, I called and was given a private tutor through them. We hit it off—and I'm still studying today.

People come to LVA for all kinds of reasons. Some can't read, and want to learn to read books to their children. Others come in because they want to get a driver's license and they need to read to take the test. Each tutor has a different student, and each student has a different goal. There are millions of Americans who need this kind of help. One out of every five adults in this country is functionally illiterate—which means they can't read and write well enough to fill out a job application or read the sports page in the newspaper.

It didn't take me long to realize that I wanted to give something back to LVA, too. When they asked me to be a student board member, I was so flattered. I didn't know anything about what that meant. But I wanted to give it a try because they had helped me so much.

I believe you have to give back to other people. I do a lot of volunteer work because I want my boys to understand that nobody is here on a free pass. We have to help each other. Sometimes that just means smiling at a guy sitting on a park bench and saying hello. That way you acknowledge he's there. Other times it means committing your time to help someone on a weekly basis.

So I said I would be a student board member of LVA. Once I got started on the board, I found out I was able to help people. I made my phone number available through the LVA newsletter, and people know they can call me in complete confidentiality. Sometimes people just want to talk. Other times, they're ready to start working with a tutor right away, and I can help them get set up with someone.

To let people know about the problem of illiteracy and what can be done to solve it, I speak at organizations and conferences—including an LVA conference in Houston where I met President George Bush and Mrs. Barbara Bush. I want people to know they shouldn't be afraid of letting people know they can't read. They shouldn't be embarrassed. I hope that if they see what I can do now, they'll see they can do it, too.

I also take the opportunity to talk to schoolteachers through volunteer work in my children's schools. I know how to pick up the signs that a child is having trouble at home—signs that teachers sometimes miss.

When my older son was in kindergarten, I had lunch with him at school as many days as I could. One day there was a little boy who brought a sandwich to school for lunch, but nothing else. He kept looking at the lunch my son and I were eating.

"Can I have that banana?" he finally asked. He could see that my son wasn't going to eat it.

"Sure," I said. "Here, have some cookies, too."

But the teacher heard us talking and came over. "We don't share food in here," she said to me. "It's against the rules."

After school, I went up to talk to her. "This child is still hungry," I said. "Can you please check and see if there's a problem at home? Maybe his parents can't afford to buy him lunches. If they can't, please let me know. I'll be glad to buy him lunches or send him some food."

If I can befriend some child, maybe he or she will see there is a different side of life. Maybe that will give them the strength to go on, no matter what they're going through.

These days, in addition to helping out LVA, I'm still working with a tutor to learn spelling and writing. I've worked really hard on spelling, but it's still so hard for me to get. That's a real handicap for me because I have so much I want to express.

My dream is to one day write a book about the story of my life—to write it for my children. It's a big project, and it won't be easy to do. But I know I can achieve it if I just keep working.

Share Donna's dream. Reach out and help someone increase his or her personal freedom. Increase literacy for adults and their families in your own community by contacting: Literacy Volunteers of America, Inc., 635 James Street, Syracuse, New York 13203. Tel: 315-472-0001. Fax: 315-472-0002. E-mail: lvanat@aol.com. Web site: **www.literacyvolunteers.org.**

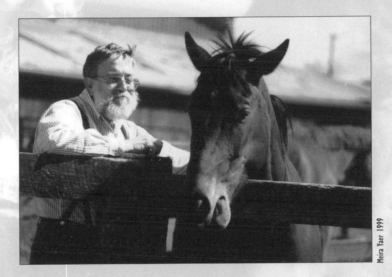

CHAPTER 5

Meira Yaer 1999

Always a Teacher

RICHARD PICKERING

I GUESS I HAVE ALWAYS BEEN A TEACHER. I used to be a teacher of art. And now, I guess I'm a teacher and a student of life. I see things now that I never saw before. I can communicate now in ways I never could before. I understand people, and animals, a lot better than I did before.

Now I learn new things all the time. I talk to people whom others pass right by. But I stop and talk for a while, and I always learn something from them. In my old life, I used to *have* to do things. Now I *get* to do them. Everything is a learning opportunity these days. That's what a brain tumor can do for you. _____

In 1989, I was a ceramics instructor and the assistant head of the Department of Fine Arts at the University of Oregon in Eugene. I worked mostly in clay myself. I made pitchers, bowls, coffee cups, and dishes.

I was married then to Rebecca. She was a researcher in the biology department. My son Tyler was about a year old, and my daughter Madeline hadn't been born yet.

I would say I was basically a happy guy, maybe just slightly depressed. But I loved teaching, and I loved my students. I especially loved the freshmen because they were always so eager to learn. I loved my graduate classes, too. They were harder to teach, but the students were so curious about everything. I like curiosity.

My students and I talked about everything together. It felt like I spent about ninety hours at school every week. We talked about the philosophy of life and poetry. I lived in the moment.

I would meet my students two nights a week, from 7 P.M. until midnight. We had a big workshop where they could weld or do anything else they wanted to do. And I always got there early so I could set everything up.

One day, when I was driving to school, I was backing down a street, and my vision got blurry. I thought it was time to go have an eye exam and get some glasses that work. But something was odd about the eye exam. The person who was giving it kept saying, "OK, let's take a break." So we would take a break, but then the test would be odd again. Finally, he told me to have an MRI.

When the MRI was finished, there were seven people standing around looking at the screen. The doctor told me I had a huge brain tumor. I cried. My wife was having a party at home. The doctor called to tell her the news.

The tumor was so big that only one doctor in the country was willing to try surgery on it. He said I had a fifty-fifty chance to come out of the surgery OK. I took the chance. The surgery took fourteen hours. They were able to get most of it out, but some of it is still in there. That means I have an MRI twice a year.

After the surgery, I was doing well at first. But then I had a brain bleed. I went into a coma, and it took me three weeks to wake up. When I woke up, I was suffering from brain damage. I didn't know that I had been asleep for three weeks. I couldn't imagine how I got so much mail overnight. I couldn't walk and I could barely talk. I didn't recognize people.

I had a very short rehab program in the hospital, but when I came home, I didn't have any formal rehab. I learned to walk again because I wanted to. It took me five months to learn. I would practice around the house. A friend of mine who had been a graduate student came over to help. We paid her to help me walk, write, speak, and learn to ride in a car again—it really frightened me to ride in a car.

I see myself as an image of a human brain. There's a devil and an angel in there. Before, the devil was taking up most of the room and coming to the front. But after my surgery, I feel like the angel came forward and gave the devil a little bit of a kick in the butt. The devil could handle a lot of hard situations. The angel is very slow at those situations. But the angel can do things the devil couldn't do. The angel can cry. I cry a lot. Before the tumor, I only cried once—I hid in a closet when I cried that one time.

There was an old Dick. And then there was a new Dick. Both of them were curious and interested in things, but from different places.

After the surgery, I was very depressed at first. I kept a journal with pictures I cut out of magazines. I put a lot of Einsteins in there, many Einsteins. I could barely write. I thought it was pointless to stay alive. Everyone was afraid I would commit suicide. They took all the knives, forks, and everything else that was sharp out of the house. Nobody knew I had a heavy-duty pistol in a drawer, underneath my socks. But I never did do that. I was just too curious. I was always thinking, "What will happen if I do stay alive?"

My wife Rebecca took my journal to a therapist named Meira Yaer, and I began to see her. She was a psychologist, though she didn't seem like one. We met once a week for a long time. I was struggling on so many levels, and part of me just wanted to give up. But mostly, I was fascinated with life. Meira and I spent most of our time talking about the beauty of life and how, in a funny way, struggles are opportunities.

I was the first person Meira worked with who had a brain injury. So, in a way, she was learning while I was learning things, too. We were both teaching and we were both learning, too. I like that.

Meira decided that if there were others I could share stories with about brain injuries, it would help me. So we started the Healing Bridge Group. Three other people and I started the group. Every time someone was willing to tell their story, I learned a lot. More people kept coming. Meira and I are still working together to help people with brain injuries.

While working with Meira, I was also learning other things. For one thing, I learned I could understand animals a lot better than I could before. I first knew that when I saw the boxer.

Near my house there is an alley with a big sign saying, "Beware. Beware. Beware." The family who lives there has a big boxer dog. And the boxer would bark and bark. It annoyed the hell out of me that this boxer would bark at me all the time. One day I thought, "Wait a minute. Maybe if the boxer got to know me, he wouldn't bark at me so much." So I slowly got to know him.

By two or three months later, I would just open that gate and go inside, and the boxer and I would lie on the ground, and I would give him a pat and scratch him. I do that all the time now with dogs. Dogs are really wild about me now, and I always carry dog treats in my pocket.

I think animals' intelligence is much higher than we think. I learned that with Ripple, Meira's horse. I just went and sat down in the middle of Ripple's pasture, and Ripple came over and laid down there with me. And we just talked a little bit. Ripple didn't judge me. And I thought that since she accepted me, maybe I could accept myself, too. People sometimes don't want to look at me because I have one eye sewn shut, but the animals all like me.

I've learned to see a lot of things differently. Behind the Sacred Heart Hospital is a big Dumpster, and I always like to look in there. I take things out of it. I took out a thing they used for hauling around an oxygen tank. I put carpeting on the place where you rest your arms, and then I used it to haul my kids around. I put my kids in it and go for walks all over Eugene. Someone threw it away because they didn't know what it could be. But when I saw it, I knew.

Sometimes sad things happen, too. One day, I got the courage to go in a car and ride to the grocery store. One of my graduate students saw me and came over to the car. I had helped him move a big sculpture one time to the people he had sold it to. I mean, it was huge. We had to get a trailer. It was a big job.

But when he saw me in the car that day, he said to me, "Well, you've been turned into a retarded person."

It disappointed me so much that that was his view of me. When we got to the grocery store, I went and found an aisle where there were no people whatsoever, sat on the floor, and cried.

I do sculpture a lot now. There's a kind of tree in Eugene that I can't think of the name of. Every time the city cuts one down, I get a piece of it and make a sculpture. They all look different. I call them "Maturity." I have forty or fifty of those now. Every one of them is different. It's like people. No two people are alike. But we're all similar.

I do hammer sculptures now, too. The hammers all start out the same. Like people. But the hammers have all been used in different ways. Some of them are chipped here, others are chipped there. The handles are different, too. I had an exhibit. People's reactions were wonderful. Their reactions were really my payment for that show.

I try to help people, like Meira helped me, whenever I can. We started out with a support group to help each other. Now we have the Healing Bridge Advocacy and Teaching Panel Group. With this group, I go around and help other people learn about brain injuries. And I talk to the speech and language students at the university. I tell them not to be judgmental. Curiosity works better than judgment. If you're judgmental, you will miss the fact that errors are wonderful because we learn a lot from them. Errors teach as much as perfection.

And I belong to another group, too, for professional people with brain injuries. I like to help out at the nursing home, and wherever people need someone to see things in a different way.

One day, Meira, her therapy dog, and I went to visit Meira's friend, a case manager at a nursing home. I met a guy there named George. He had a brain injury and was incredibly grumpy sometimes. He didn't have anybody. I made some Play-Doh with him. We took some wheels, and George just moved them around on the Play-Doh and made different shapes. I liked that. And I found out that George played the piano. No one else knew it at that place. No one else tried to find out what George could do. They didn't really see him—but I did.

I also go to a group where people have had strokes. There's a man there who had a severe stroke. He could not speak at all. I drew pictures with him on the blackboard. I liked that. I work mainly in sculpture. But still, I like drawing, too. So we drew a lot. And now he can speak.

I wish I could do some of the things I could do before. But I like myself more now. I feel like I've learned a lot. I know about dealing with difficulties now. And I have a lot more to learn and to teach. Educating others about brain injury is so important. We are all different and we are all the same. Every person has a right to be accepted.

I used to be a teacher. People say I still am.

Help others with brain injury realize their potential. Learn how to turn a support group into an advocacy and teaching panel and much more. Contact: Brain Injury Training & Services, Inc., c/o Opening The Way, Inc., 16209 Del Malley, Dallas, Texas 75248.

Jonni Angel

JONNI McKENZIE McCUIN

A S FAR BACK AS I CAN REMEMBER, I can't ever recall being happy until I finally asked God to take control of my life. Before that, I just barely struggled along. As a child and young adult, my life just went from one crisis to the next. Then one day, I told God that I just didn't see any point in living any more. I told Him that if He wanted me to live, He was going to have to help me figure out how to do it.

And God was right there for me. All I'd had to do was ask.

The suffering in my life started when I was little.

One night when I was ten years old, my brothers and I were home alone (we lived with our mother) when one of my uncles came over. My father never came to see me, but my uncles came around a lot. They would come over to my house to drink with my mother.

This particular night, my mother was at work, and my brothers and I were playing with a cigarette she had left in the ashtray. I was just starting to smoke it when my uncle walked in and caught me.

"Well, you know you're going to get a whipping," my uncle said. I started crying. I had seen my mama whip my brothers and I knew I didn't want that. My uncle said he wouldn't tell Mama if I went home with him.

When we got to his house, he pulled out something that looked like a cigarette, but he rolled it up differently. I didn't know it was marijuana. He told me to smoke it. When I tried it, I decided it was better than a cigarette.

And then he began to fondle me. I knew it was wrong for my uncle to touch me that way. But I was more afraid of getting a whipping than I was of having him touch me. So I let him do it.

At the time, I was skinny and gawky and everyone teased me. But I found one group of kids that would accept me—if I brought them weed from my uncle. So this was the crowd I started to hang with.

It was also around that time that one of my uncles gave me my first beer. I drank the whole thing straight down. It gave me an absolutely sensational feeling. I felt braver. I felt stronger. I felt like no one could harm me—or if they did, I wouldn't care. By the time I was thirteen, I could drink eight cans of beer in one sitting.

My younger brother was drinking a lot, too. One night, he got so drunk and sick, I had to put him in the tub and wash him off. I guess we were up pretty late that night, because when Mama came home from work the next morning, we had overslept for school. So she whipped us.

The whipping mama gave us that morning crossed the line into abuse. I still have the scars from that day—scars from where Mama cut my arms with glass. I wore a long-sleeved shirt to school that day. And when I got there, I used a pay phone to call the courthouse. I told them I didn't want to live with my mother any more. They told me my only other choice was the juvenile hall. I chose that over staying at home.

The police came to school to pick me up and took me to a shelter. After they took pictures of my arms, they went back to school to get my brother. And then they sent me to a place called the Sunshine Home.

At the Sunshine Home, I immediately found the kids who were doing drugs and alcohol. I did anything to numb the constant pain and confusion, the loneliness. I had no one to turn to—no mama, no father, no brothers. I wondered why I had ever been put on this earth.

Before long, I got into trouble at the Sunshine Home. And when I did, I overheard the owner saying, "Well, that little nigger troublemaker is never going to succeed anyway."

I figured he was right. So I ran away. I went to live with a friend and her grandmother in the West Dallas projects, and from there I enrolled myself in school. I remembered a teacher saying one time, "The only thing you can have that nobody can take away from you is an education." So I tried to do well in school.

Then one day, I was late for class and got called to the principal's office. He said he was going to give me five licks for being late and that I had to stand perfectly still the whole time. He told me that if I moved at all, he would start all over again. I stayed perfectly still for the first four licks. But it hurt so bad, I moved before the fifth lick. So he started over.

That's when something just snapped inside me. I just couldn't take any more pain. I turned to the principal and went at him with a pen.

They kicked me out of school.

At eighteen, I joined the Navy, thinking that would help me put my life together. But because I was still drinking and doing drugs, I managed to get in trouble and stay in trouble. I left the Navy with a dishonorable discharge—and a baby on the way.

When my son Jonathan was born, I came back to Dallas, back to the projects. I loved my son and wanted to stay clean for him. I really did. But I was in pain when I was clean, and in pain when I used. So it just didn't seem to matter that I stop.

Then on one Thursday, after four straight days of doing drugs, I just couldn't see any reason to live any longer. I went to the bathroom and looked myself in the mirror.

I said, "God, whoever you are, God, wherever you are, I am miserable. And I never heard of God wanting one of His children to be miserable. Please could you just let me die?"

And I told God my plan about killing myself. "I'm going to drink and drink until Sunday," I told Him. "If I'm dead on Sunday, that's good. If I'm not, I'll take that as a sign that You'll show me how to be happy."

And I drank.

On Saturday night at midnight, when I realized I was still alive, I said to God, "OK, what are you telling me?"

Right that minute, I started to feel different. That minute was the turning point in my life. Right then, I got down on my knees and prayed.

I went to a treatment facility for two weeks, and something inside of me just kept telling me everything was going to be all right. But it was so hard. When I got out, I realized that everyone around me was doing drugs and drinking. I could just feel their misery.

And I knew I had to turn to God. I realized He was the only one who could help me.

"I don't know what to do," I told Him. "If you don't do something right this minute, I'm going to walk out this door and start getting high all over again because I just don't know what else to do."

And that's when the phone rang. It was another addict in my support group from the treatment center wanting to talk. But I knew it wasn't the person talking to me—I knew it was God. I knew I had finally made contact.

I've let go of so many things since then. I haven't used drugs since I left the treatment center. And I haven't even had the desire to use drugs since that phone call.

When I first became clean, I said, "God, you helped me get off drugs. Now let me run the rest of my life." But every time I tried to run my life without God's guidance, I got into trouble. So I slowly gave God a little bit more and a little bit more of myself.

And what I know now is that God doesn't meet me halfway. God is there *all* the way, *all* the time. It's up to me to reach out and make that connection. And since I've asked for God's help, I've been able to make peace in so many aspects of my life. So much of my life has changed. I've finished school, and I've mended a lot of fences. And I met my husband.

Actually, he was someone I had met years earlier. I was a little girl then, and he was ten years older than me. Even so, I had a major crush on him. Then, when I entered a twelve-step program for support after my treatment, I walked into the first meeting and there he was. We both worked really hard in recovery, and we started seeing each other. We married in 1992.

Since my recovery, I've been able to reconnect with my mother. God has helped me realize that she was doing the best she knew how. We're not really close, and I don't rely on her for anything, but I do see her. We've talked about the time the police came and took me away, and to this day she says the whipping she gave me was not abuse. But I'm firm and calm in my understanding of what happened. I tell her she may have been tired from work all night, she may have had rent due and no money—but yes, it was abuse. And I forgive her. I often tell her I love her. I've even forgiven my uncle for taking such terrible advantage of me. I've learned that however I choose to be—whether it's vengeful or forgiving—that's the way *I'm* going to be feeling inside. Not how anyone else is going to be feeling.

I believe that God kept me alive for a reason. I tried to drink myself to death that weekend, but God had a different plan for me. And everything I went through before that, all the pain and suffering, is a learning experience that I am benefiting from. Because of my own suffering, I now have compassion and empathy for people. And a deep desire to help.

Not too long after God helped me turn my life around, a friend called to ask if I could work two hours a week at a treatment program called Our Brother's Keeper. And I said I would. As soon as I started working there, I knew this was the place I was meant to be. Now I work there full-time.

Our Brother's Keeper is a treatment center for teenagers from the same area of town I grew up in. I know these kids. I know their pain. I know what drove them to drinking and drugging in the first place. Other people might look at them and think they're worthless. But when I look at them, I see scared, angry, misunderstood kids. Some of these kids have never had anyone who believes in them, anyone who understands their pain. But I do. And they know it.

I know that's what I'm on this earth to do right now—to help the kids in the program believe in themselves and their future. I even hope to open my own drug treatment center one day.

In many ways, I treat these kids the same way I treat my own son. Jonathan is fourteen now, and I have been completely honest with him about my life. I've taken him to counseling with me. I've told him the truth, so he would be able to make better choices than I did. He's a wonderful boy and he's doing great.

When the teens in the treatment program talk to me, they know I'm going to tell them the truth, just like I do for my own son. And when I tell them they can make it, they can look at me and know that's the truth.

The other day, a teenage girl came in. As she sat across from me, I saw myself— the anger, the pain, the loneliness. I hugged her and held her in my arms. And as I let her know she was loved, I gave thanks to God.

I know who I am, and I know why I'm here. And I will always be thankful for that.

"Jonni Angels" are everywhere, anxious to give back. If you are an angel in waiting, let Jonni get you going in your own community. For those who are grateful for centers of recovery, perpetuate their success by getting involved. Contact: Our Brother's Keeper NDUGU, Inc., 4200 South Fitzhugh Avenue, Dallas, Texas 75210-1103. Tel: 214-421-7671.

CHAPTER 7

Susan Kandell 1999

A Bald Head to Kiss

DEB GREER

MOST PARENTS WOULD AGREE IT'S HARD to imagine anything worse than a child with a life-threatening disease—with the exception, of course, of actually losing that child. As parents, you hear about children's hospitals filled with these sick kids, and you just hope and pray you'll never see the inside of one. But that's exactly where my husband and I found ourselves when our son, Jason, was twelve years old.

Today, it's a world we would never willingly leave. Because it is there—among those heartsick parents and frightened children—that we are able to share the blessings of the love that came our way when our own needs, too, were so great.

My son Jason was always an active child, and a tough one. He played football and basketball, and loved the physical nature of games. And, like all fifth-graders in sports, he got bumped and bruised a lot. So I didn't pay too much attention in the spring of 1991 when he started complaining that this hurt and that hurt. Then one day, while he was wrestling with my brother, he suddenly dropped to the floor in pain. And when he took off his shirt, we saw a small bump on the top of his shoulder.

At our pediatrician's suggestion, we took him to an orthopedic doctor who said it might be a separated or broken bone that would heal on its own. He thought we should just watch it for a bit.

With that diagnosis, we went ahead with our plans for spring break. My husband Jeff, a minister with the International Foundation in Missoula, Montana, and I had been taking a group of kids to do community service work during spring break for several years. It grew out of the work we had done with teens for years through an organization called Young Life. That year, we took the group to Tijuana, Mexico, to paint an orphanage. And, of course, we took Jason and our other son, Jonathan, a seventh-grader at the time, with us, too.

During the week we were in Mexico, the bump on Jason's shoulder grew from the size of a pea to the size of a golf ball. When we got back to Missoula, Jason was hospitalized for a biopsy. Afterward, the doctor met us in the waiting room. When he spoke to us, our old life ended.

"Jeff and Deb, I have the worst news," he said. "We believe Jason has cancer. You need to get him to a major medical center quickly. We recommend taking him to Seattle." We asked a few questions, but our shock prevented us from completely hearing his answers. All we really knew was that we needed to be with Jason.

Jason's only fear right then was that he didn't want to be left alone in the hospital, and we promised him he wouldn't be; so either Jeff or I was with him every minute of the day. When Jeff was with Jason, I would spend my time just sobbing until I had to go back in the room.

In those first few days, I could barely figure out how to put one foot in front of the other. I heard words, but I couldn't sort them out. I felt like I was sitting in a dunking booth, and someone had hit the bull's-eye. I was suddenly under water and my only choices were either drowning or swimming to the top. I wanted to get out all together—but getting out wasn't an option.

When Jason came home from the hospital, our house was filled with friends and family. We visited with everyone while we packed up our family and my parents packed up their motor home. Within a few days, we arrived at Seattle Children's Hospital. Jeff and Jonathan and I lived in the Ronald McDonald House, while Mom and Dad parked their motor home in the lot next door. That was our home base for almost two months.

One of my most traumatic moments happened during the first days we were in Seattle. Jason had to have some minor surgery before they could start his treatment, so we were in the waiting room at the hospital. And all these little bald-headed kids with tubes coming out of every possible place were running around. It was so frightening to me—like a scene out of *The Twilight Zone*. I was constantly thinking, "What am I doing here? Why am I in this scene?"

I had the feeling that if I could just get away from all these bald heads and all these tubes and bags and machines—that if I could just get away from it all, then my child wouldn't really be sick.

We were so lost those first few days. The hospital itself is a maze, an enormous teaching hospital. We literally didn't know where we were. Plus, we didn't understand the language that was being spoken—the language of pediatric cancer. We didn't know the protocols, the rules, the regulations. We had been dropped down in the middle of this new culture, and we were just completely lost.

But in the midst of such mental and emotional chaos, our lives were forever changed by the kindness of strangers. Two sets of seasoned parents who had survived the trauma of this adjustment quietly took us under their wings. The women showed us where to find the chairs that made into beds, so one of us could always sleep in the room with Jason. They showed us where they kept the blankets and how to find the kitchen, so we could make a snack for Jason whenever he needed it.

I was feeling so fragile, like a thin piece of glass that was already cracked and could shatter into a million pieces at the slightest wrong touch. But these parents were so gentle. We were strangers to them, but they just wrapped us in their love from the very beginning. They knew exactly what we needed.

And their sons did the same for Jason. Chad and Eric, both bald as billiard balls, were as friendly as kids could get. They became Jason's immediate new best friends.

Jason's treatment lasted for eighteen months, and he saw Chad and Eric on and off for the first several months of that time. We would go to Seattle to have the doctors start a round of chemotherapy. We'd stay out there for a while to see how Jason was doing, how he was reacting to it, and then we'd go home to finish the round.

Chemotherapy is never easy. This poison they put in your body to kill the cancer doesn't make the rest of your body real happy either. There are side effects and there are complications. And Jason had his share. But overall, he seemed to be responding to the treatment, and we were so grateful.

But even with Jason's progress, it took me a very long time to get over the feeling that this whole existence was just a waking nightmare. I found it impossible to believe that the rest of the world was just going on around us—as if nothing had changed.

I remember one day when I was driving next to a huge truck. And I looked up at the trucker and I thought, "You idiot. How can you just drive along thinking everything is OK. Don't you know that it's not OK? Don't you even know that the whole entire world has fallen apart?"

And then, within five months of Jason's having met Eric and Chad, both of these lovely boys died.

We were in Seattle when Eric died. The day before, he and Jason spent some time together. And at one point, their eyes really caught, and Eric said to Jason, "You'll be OK. You're going to make it." Jason felt like that was his personal prophecy. He just hung onto it. Both he and Chad left the hospital to be at Eric's service.

Then within one week in September, Chad's one tumor turned into seventeen, and he called us in Missoula from Seattle. "I think I'm going pretty fast," he said. "Are you guys going to come out again?" So we loaded everyone in the motor home and drove to Seattle.

I believe that losing Chad was the hardest thing Jason ever went through—more difficult for him than his own chemo. I remember him laying his little head on the bed next to Chad's and sobbing. And we all felt just like Jason did.

In the middle of Jason's treatment, about six months after Chad's death, we took Jason and Jonathan with an organization called Operation Care Lift to bring Christmas to children's hospitals in Moscow. Our group took thousands of teddy bears to the children on the cancer floors. I don't know whether it was the bears or Jason's bald head that broke the language barrier, but it was a wonderful trip, filled with love.

I think going to Russia and reaching out to those other children healed Jason as much as the chemo. It was the most healing thing we all did during his treatment. The opportunity to give freely to others helped us to focus less on our own pain. That trip also gave us a wonderful chance to spend some time with Jonathan. Like so many siblings of cancer patients, Jonathan had a struggle all his own—a struggle to understand, to fit in. It was difficult for him, but in Russia, we all had a wonderful time together.

A third friend of Jason's, a little girl named Jessie, died a few years after Eric and Chad. We were with her when she died, and we all went to the outdoor memorial service together. But just as we all gathered under the little tent to sit down, Jason started to shake and sob.

Carol, Jesse's mom, got up from where she was sitting, came over to Jason, and took him over to one of the vans parked nearby. They sat together, and she talked him through it. And then they came back, and this woman proceeded on with the memorial service for her daughter.

It was absolutely an enigma to me. How can you be at your own daughter's funeral and care about my child in the middle of it? This is the kind of love we were dealing with from these parents.

It was these children's deaths—Eric, Chad, and Jessie—that really led me to a crisis of faith. My faith had always been such a big part of my life. We routinely shared Christ with high school kids, speaking of the God we loved so much. But in my new upside-down life, I was facing a heavenly father who had the power to stop childhood disease and death, but chose not to. What kind of a God is that?

I finally cried out to God, just for some understanding. And, uniquely enough, it really came to me through the love I shared with these other parents. And through Jason. "Mom, you can never doubt God," Jason said to me once. "If nothing else, we know there is a heaven. We watched our friends go there."

And Jason taught me that I had been looking at it all backward. I had convinced myself that if I believed in God, He would protect me and always help me out at every crisis in my life. But Scripture never says that. Scripture says that life is hard. "It rains on the just and unjust" (Matthew 5:45). Our faith, no matter how strong it is, does not protect us from that. We are glad that Jesus is always there to walk us through it. I do believe we are a living example of that.

Of all the children we came to love in Seattle, Jason is the only one who survived. But the parents of those children are now our very best friends. And it is the love we share with them that now directs our lives.

No one knows more what it means to have someone to sit with you, love you, and guide you through the maze of pediatric cancer than Jeff and I. And that is what we have given our lives over to. I don't even know exactly when it happened, but we made the decision just to be available for families in similar circumstances. Our own kids are in college now—Jason is going to school in Hawaii, taking a much-needed break from what goes on around here—so Jeff and I do have the freedom to just pick up and go. And that's what we do.

Together with friends, we helped start an organization called Side by Side, under the umbrella of the International Foundation. We do have to spend some time raising funds, but we spend most of our time counseling cancer families, walking them through the experience, whenever and wherever they need us. Right now, it's just Jeff and I and two young men we trained who are working in Seattle. We hope it will grow, because we know firsthand how many people need this kind of support.

If someone calls us, we get in the car and go. If there's a family in western Montana with a child who needs help, we're there for them. We get calls in the middle of the night, on holidays—whenever someone needs us. It fills our life with purpose to know that we can be there for these families. We received so much love when our own son was sick. And we plan to spend the rest of our lives passing that love around.

It's funny. You know, when we first came to Seattle, all these little ones with the bald heads were so frightening to us. They represented this terrible disease, and we just didn't want to believe it was part of Jason's life. But now, when we go to

Seattle to be with another family, the first thing we do is look for one of those little bald heads to kiss.

Help Deb give support to others in need. Contact: The International Foundation, P. O. Box 23813, c/o Servant Leadership, Washington D.C. 20026-3813.

Susan Kandell 1999

An Aura of Strength

BRIANNE SCHWANTES

EVEN WHEN I WAS IN MY MOTHER'S WOMB, the doctors knew something was wrong with me. The ultrasound picture they had made of me didn't show any bones. The doctors didn't tell my parents about it, though, because there wasn't anything they could have done about it.

Those doctors feared the worst. But as far as I'm concerned, they got the best. Yes, I'm short, and, yes, I'm frail. And I've been through more broken bones and surgeries than you could imagine. But I wouldn't trade the life I've had for anything in the world—not even good health. It's just been way too much fun just the way it is. _____

I was born with thirteen broken bones. I had already broken my arms and my legs, and my skull wasn't fully formed. The doctors told my parents they didn't know exactly what was wrong with me, but they didn't think I was going to make it through that first night. In fact, before I was two weeks old, I had been baptized and given last rites three times.

At that point, my parents were advised to put me in an institution and just leave me there. The doctors never thought I'd make it to preschool—much less carry a backpack around at the University of Wisconsin, where I am now. But my parents never even considered institutionalizing me. They said I was their child, and they were going to do what they thought was right for me.

So my whole extended family started calling all over the world to find someone who would know something about this rare disease I apparently had. And they ended up at the National Institutes of Health in Washington DC, finding a doctor who said I had osteogenesis imperfecta (OI).

OI is a disease in which the bones grow, but not well. They're very fragile. When I was little, even hiccuping would cause me to break my ribs. If someone pushed me, I would break my arm. One time my dad reached around from the driver's seat to the back seat of the car, and broke my jaw just by accidentally hitting me with his elbow.

Since my initial diagnosis as an infant, I've been to the NIH to see my doctor every three months for my entire life. I see her and other specialists, and then have X-rays, CAT scans, MRIs, blood draws, and anything else you could think of. They had me in long steel braces from the time I was a baby until I was twelve. And they've tried many different drugs and different protocols to see if this would work or that would work, if it would make me grow or strengthen my bones.

Nothing has really worked, in terms of helping my bones. But everything the doctors did for me helped to strengthen my muscles. And that is definitely one of the reasons I can do as much as I can today.

My parents have also worked my whole life to help me get strong and live as normal a life as possible. When I was just a few weeks old, for example, my mom already had me in the pool at the YMCA, giving me exercise.

One day, when I was six weeks old and in the pool with her, a woman just started screaming in front of everyone and ran over to us. My mother was so embarrassed. This woman said, "Your daughter has the best aura I have ever seen. She is just glowing. I can feel it all the way across the pool."

My mom was kind of taken aback. She didn't really believe in auras and all that stuff. But when I heard the story, I felt like that woman was saying, "This child has a gift. She's cool." And that was a premonition about my life.

When I got a little older, my parents would dress me in a sweatshirt, sweatpants, socks, and shoes before putting me in the pool. That way, they figured, I would strengthen my muscles because I'd have to work harder to swim. When I refused to walk, they spread beads on the floor so it would be uncomfortable for me to crawl. I might not have enjoyed it all at the time, but everything my parents did for me helped me to become the strong person I am today.

The first time I remember noticing that I was different from other children was in kindergarten. They always played tag and hide and seek. But I couldn't play those games because I could break a bone or get knocked out if I did.

Instead, I invented this game called "Dogs," where we would all crawl around and play like we were different dogs. The other kids loved it, and we played it for months. Eventually, we were forced to stop because parents called the school to say they were tired of their kids crawling around all the time. But the experience helped me realize that just because I couldn't do what the other kids were doing didn't mean I couldn't invent something else great to do.

When I started in elementary school, my parents were so nervous about my bones breaking that they enlisted the help of two women who came to school with me every day. So until I was a freshman in high school, I went to school with bodyguards. I didn't really mind, though, because they were so nice. One of the women used to be an elementary school teacher, so she would come and home-school me whenever I was out with broken bones. She became a good friend.

I broke so many bones in elementary school. And it hurt so much. It hurts just as much for me to break a bone as for anyone else. It's just that when your bones break so often, you have to learn to get over it fast. So I forced myself to learn how to deal with the pain.

It always seemed that just when things were going well, another bone would break. When I was in elementary school, I noticed a kind of rule that has held true for my life. Whenever I have two good things happen, one bad thing happens. It's just always been that way for me. As soon as two great things happen, I always break a bone or have some other kind of problem.

But I don't let it bother me. I never let myself get into the depth of despair. I always look for something good. I can always say, "OK, so I did break my back. But I can still read a good book. I can still play with my cat."

My mother developed the best system to help me get through all those broken bones. Each time I had to get another cast on, I would be so depressed. She'd let me cry for a bit, and then she'd say, "OK, Brianne. Here's what we're going to do. For the first two weeks, we'll just sit on the couch and watch TV and let your bone start to heal. Then, for the next two weeks, we'll get a tutor to help you start catching up with school. And after that, we'll help you get back to school a bit at a time."

We went through that cycle so many times. And each time I would reach a new low, my parents would make a plan of action for me. It helped me so much to see a goal I could reach toward. By the time I got to high school, I could take the broken bones more in stride. By then, I knew who my friends were. I knew they cared about me for who I was, and I knew that broken bones weren't going to change that.

But even now, every time I break a bone, I think, "Oh, my God. It's going to be the stupid cast again, and six months more of physical therapy, back in a wheelchair, back on crutches—all over again."

And again, when I get down to my lowest point, my family is always there for me. My mom and dad say, "Come on, Brianne. Suck it up. You gotta keep going." And of course, they're right.

For a while, I was having a bad problem with my jaw, and could just barely eat. That was the worst time. I'm so small as it is—I'm 4'6" and weigh only about sixty pounds or so. But with this jaw problem, I was down to fifty pounds. When I'd get out of the shower and look at myself in the mirror, I would just start to cry. One time, I just sank to the floor sobbing. I couldn't help it. And my mother came in and we cried together. I missed a lot of school that year because it was just so awful not to be able to eat.

But when I went into the hospital for surgery to fix my jaw, I saw these kids who were in so much worse shape than I was. Then I thought, "How can I possibly be depressed when I'm walking around and I'm virtually normal and I have my independence? How can I be depressed over that little thing in my life when other people are in such bad shape?"

Sure, there have been times when I've been tempted to question God or feel like He is punishing me for some reason I don't understand. There have been times when I've wondered why this had to happen. But then I think about all the wonderful things that have happened in my life, and I know I can't really stay depressed.

From the time I was little, one of the things that has always made me feel the best has been helping other people with their problems. It's always been very healing for me.

Even when I was very young, when I would go see my doctor at NIH, I would always encourage the other kids with OI. They all looked up to me because I am the one in our group at NIH who can walk the most. The doctors don't even know why I can walk, because looking at the MRIs and everything, it doesn't seem like it should be possible. But I just made up my mind and I did it.

So whenever I would see the other kids with OI, I would tell them to wear their braces, to do their exercises, to do what the doctors told them. I wanted all of us to do the best we could. And when I was encouraging them, it really made me feel better, too.

I try to help people with OI whenever I can. A lot of people with OI can't even leave their homes because they're in such bad shape. I've e-mailed a girl named Amber, who has OI too. She has been able to walk at different times throughout her life, but not continuously. I keep writing her and encouraging her and telling her to never give up. I told her that there were times when I felt like I could never walk again, too—but I kept trying anyway.

When I was thirteen, there were all these terrible floods in the Midwest. I kept hearing about them on TV, and I just really wanted to do something to help those poor people. I didn't want to just send money. I wanted to be there, to let them know I cared.

So I begged my parents. And we went. There was a group of college kids and my mother and dad and my sister Liz, and we all drove to Iowa to help. My dad spent the week working with a big sump pump to suck all the muck out of people's basements. Mom and Liz helped bring food and water to elderly people. And I stayed in the relief center and sorted donations.

My doctors thought I was crazy to go. I could have so easily broken a bone in that situation. And I knew that. But so many people have helped me. How could I not give back to people who needed it? To me, it was simple. These people needed help, so I went.

One day on that trip, I was sitting next to a man on a curb in Des Moines, while we were waiting for the Salvation Army food truck. The man offered me his fruit roll-up, and we started to talk. He seemed really nice, and it turns out he was Tony Rodham, President Clinton's brother-in-law. The next time I went to Washington to see my doctor, we got a phone call from the White House. President Clinton wanted to meet with me! So I met President Clinton in the Oval Office, which was very, very cool.

Three months later, I got another phone call from the White House. The President was requesting my family's presence in Denver, where the Pope was coming to meet people for World Youth Day. We stood on the rope lines, and the Pope came over to us first and blessed us. He blessed me, then he blessed Liz and shook my parents' hands. My mother had billions of rosaries for him to bless. It was very cool. There's a famous picture that was taken that day of the President pointing us out in the crowd to the Pope.

I also got to meet President and Mrs. Bush once. That came about in part because for six years, my sister and I gave testimony in the House of Representatives to try to secure more funding for NIH. We feel we contributed to the fact that the NIH—and my own health care—has more secure funding now. When it came time to dedicate the Children's Inn (which is similar to a Ronald McDonald House) at the NIH, I was chosen as a spokesperson for the kids who would be using the house. At the dedication ceremony, I met the Bushes.

Right now, I'm working through the Ambassador's Program of an organization called Heart of America. We speak to kids at schools about motivation, community service, doing your best. It makes me feel so good to do that. I know that the kids we speak to sometimes feel like they have so many problems, or like they have so little hope for their future. But I have the opportunity to show them another way to look at their lives. I have a chance to tell them what I've learned.

And it makes me feel great to know that I can make a difference.

I want all people, especially kids, to know there are no limitations to what you can do with your life. The doctors didn't think I was going to live past day one. And look at me now.

If you are a student and, like Brianne, know that anything is possible for anyone, contact: Heart of America, 201 Massachusetts Avenue NE, Suite CE, Washington D.C. 20002. Tel: 202-546-3256. Fax: 202-546-3257. E-mail: heartofamerica@erols.com. Web site: **www.heartofamerica.org.**

Susan Kandell 1999

Loved by an Angel in Fur

ALLEN ANDERSON

As a retired police officer, it's hard for me to imagine a more stressful life than that of a cop. For years, I didn't know how to deal with the stress of working on the police force in the most violent area of Atlanta. I would come home, turn off all the lights, and then sit in the dark until I could finally relax a bit. That was the only way I had of trying to escape from the madness I felt all around me. At least for those few minutes of darkness and silence, I could close out the violence. At least for those few minutes, I could close myself off from the terror.

But one day—one lucky day—I discovered a much better way to deal with my stress and my insecurities. I made that discovery in the form of a beautiful, fluffy ball of fur named Prana, whose name means "breath of life." I will never forget what that dog did for me. Now I am dedicated to sharing the beauty she brought into my life with others, and to making the world a better place with—and for—our animals.

Policework wasn't the first stressful thing I had ever done in my life. That would be my childhood. My father was in the Air Force. Since we never lived anywhere long enough for me to make real friends, I was alone much of the time. We lived in Japan, Colorado, Georgia, Louisiana, South Carolina, and Puerto Rico. It might sound exciting to live in so many different places, but it wasn't—it was lonely.

In addition, my father had a problem with alcohol. I never knew when the next violent outburst was coming. I knew it was coming—I just didn't know when. In my child's mind, I thought that if I could just be good enough, just be careful enough, my father would stop drinking. Then we would have the stable life I longed for.

As the oldest of three children, I felt a tremendous sense of responsibility as far back as I can remember. I was a child trying so hard to be an adult—always working, making money, listening to problems. Always trying to keep the violence at home from happening.

As a result, I became a closed-down, fearful person. I thought anyone I met would try to hurt me. And even if they didn't, I knew they wouldn't like me. I had no self-esteem, no sense of my own worth.

When I graduated from college, I knew I wanted to do something to help other people, to try to keep them from feeling as bad about themselves as I felt about myself. At first, I thought journalism might be the way. I wanted to work in television, where I thought I could resolve conflict by helping people see both sides of an issue. And I knew that being in front of a camera would force me to get past my own fears. But before I started my first job, I had a motorcycle accident that scarred my face. That was the end of my career as a TV reporter.

Instead, I went the police route. I worked in Atlanta, in a difficult part of town. Day after day, I dealt with people who had such severe problems, who had a victim mentality, who—like me—had no real sense of self-worth. Although I wanted to make a difference in their lives, I never felt like I was actually helping anyone. The traumas seemed never to end.

There was the day I was called out to help a woman and her boyfriend. They had just gotten off the bus in a bad part of town when a man attacked them with a butcher knife. He stabbed the boyfriend directly in the heart. As I arrived, the perpetrator was running off. I held the boyfriend in my arms as the blood oozed from his heart, and the young woman screamed hysterically. We all knew there was nothing I could do. I was looking right into this young man's eyes as he died.

Another day, I was driving down the street when an older man came out of a house and started shooting at my police car. I got out and pointed my gun at him. I started to shoot, but something inside told me to wait for a second. Just then, his wife ran out and grabbed the gun from him. As it turns out, the old man was hard of hearing and mentally not quite with it. He really didn't know what he was doing. And I had almost killed him.

Everyone I spoke to was a victim, full of pain. And I seemed to take every fear, every worry, and turn it into my own. I had gone into police work to help people avoid the pain I had felt as a child. Instead, my days seemed to be filled with nothing but pain.

I would come home at night despondent. I had nightmares continually and could barely sleep through the night. When I finally spoke to my wife about it, I was practically in tears. "It's always the same thing out there, Linda, day after day and night after night. Nothing ever gets better," I said. "It may be different faces, but they're all doing the same thing. The deaths, the wounds, the break-ins, the tears, the pain, the screams."

But then, when I wasn't sure how I could go on, Linda and I did something that turned my life around—although we didn't know it that at the time. We decided to buy a dog. When we answered the ad in the newspaper, we found a whole litter full of puppies. All of them were so cute. We couldn't choose one over the others.

"OK, listen up now," Linda told the dogs. "Whichever one of you really wants to come home with us, you're going to have to let us know." One puppy came right over and untied my shoelaces with her teeth. We named her Prana because somehow we knew she was going to give us the "breath of life" we needed.

I thought we brought Prana home as a pet for Linda, our two children, and me. But before long, I noticed something much more important, and much more wonderful.

When I came home at night, despondent over the traumas of the day, Prana would come over to me the second she saw me. She would look up into my face and wag her tail. She always looked as if she were smiling, genuinely happy to see me. Then I would get down on the floor and play with her. First, I'd scratch her behind the ears, and then on her stomach. Then she'd bring her ball over to me and bark until I took her outside to play.

When I went outside with Prana, she would come and sit right next to my feet, looking straight up at me with those adoring eyes. She never took her eyes away from my face. She made me feel like she would have been perfectly happy to just sit and stare at me for the rest of her life.

Stare at me? Allen Anderson? No one had ever thought I was that important. No one had ever loved me that way before. No one had given me the unconditional love that Prana gave me each and every night.

And what did I have to do to earn this beautiful love, this unwavering loyalty? Nothing. It didn't matter to Prana what I did. I didn't have to pretend to be anything I wasn't. She didn't care if I was great at work or terrible. She didn't care if my uniform was ironed just right or not. She didn't care how much money I made or how many commendations I got. Prana loved me just for being me. I was good enough for her, exactly the way I was. It had never occurred to me that I could be worth loving that much. In my whole life, I had never felt the power of that kind of love.

When I would look into Prana's eyes and see that love and adoration, a tremendous sense of inner peace would come over me. I was able to forget about work. I could feel the tension slipping off me. I could forget about the childhood hurts I still carried with me every day. When I was with Prana, I was in the moment, not living in the past.

When she would bark at a squirrel running above our heads, I saw the beauty of the interwoven tree branches and leaves for the first time. And when she brought the ball to me and dropped it at my feet absolutely each and every time I threw it, I learned the meaning of trust.

As much as I loved my wife and children, I can honestly say that no human being revealed the power of love to me the way Prana did. I had always felt like there was a dark spot on my heart, almost like a great wall. Nothing could come in through that wall, and nothing could really go out. But Prana's acceptance and unconditional love broke down that wall. With her help, my soul began to heal.

After spending time with Prana, I could feel my heart and soul open. And then I was able to give of myself to my wife and children the way I truly wanted to. And once I started opening up inside, I also started relating to my job differently.

In the past, I had done things strictly by the book, never really connecting with the people I came in contact with. But after Prana came into my life, if I made a drug arrest, I would ask the person, "Is this really what you want to do with your life? Is this really in your best interest?" If I were answering a call about domestic violence, I would ask the victim, "Is this a relationship you want to stay in? Is there something you could do differently? Could you prosecute this time?" I was asking these questions because I really cared.

I began to notice that animals worked a similar kind of magic for other people, too. One night I answered a domestic violence call and found a man and a woman fighting, fighting, fighting. The woman was injured, and I called an ambulance. I had the man on the floor, trying to cuff him as he struggled against me.

In the middle of this insanity, a nine-year-old boy was sitting on the couch; next to him was a short-haired mixed-breed dog calmly licking the tears from this boy's eyes. The only sane part of that entire apartment was the bubble of love the dog put around that boy. That dog was the calm, the love, the total devotion, the angel he needed.

That moment changed the direction of my whole life. I knew I wanted to spend my life sharing this idea of the deep spiritual bond between people and animals. I committed myself right then to helping people open up to the many lessons animals can teach us—lessons of acceptance, self-worth, patience, joy, playfulness, and curiosity.

With the spiritual and emotional help Prana had given me, I decided to quit police work and aim for a less stressful life. So Linda and I moved to Minneapolis, where we established Angel Animals®, an organization that helps to spread the word about the spiritual bond between animals and people.

Angel Animals® provides a forum for people to share stories about animals, supports animal shelters around the country, and raises awareness about animal abuse.

Before we started Angel Animals®, we had no idea how many people credited their animals with enhancing, or even saving, their lives. Through our newsletters and web site, hundreds of people have shared stories about dogs, cats, birds, and other animals—even insects—whose unconditional love, compassion, and intelligence have brought people from sickness to health, from depression to happiness.

Not everyone views animals the way we do, of course. Even some pet owners argue against the idea that they could have a spiritual connection with animals.

But once people really start thinking and talking about animals, that view often changes.

For example, not too long ago, Linda and I were being interviewed about Angel Animals® on a radio show. One man called up to say that his dog, Zoomie, was a nice dog, but that he wasn't emotionally—and certainly not spiritually—attached to the dog. He said he took him for walks and fed him. That was it.

"Have you learned anything from Zoomie?" I asked the man.

"Well, I've learned patience from him."

"OK, there you are. Your dog *has* taught you something."

From my view, patience is definitely a spiritual quality. Maybe this man wasn't comfortable with the word *spiritual,* but he definitely knew he was learning important values from his dog.

Animals bring people into an amazing world of love. We've heard it over and over again—too many times to doubt the power of that love.

Prana isn't with us any more. But I will never forget the beauty and love that dog brought into my life. I owe her a tremendous debt of gratitude. She opened my heart so I could see a world of love—a world more powerful than the world of violence and pain I had been living in. I hope to repay that debt by using the rest of my life to spread the word that animals can help us find the potential for love that exists within all of us.

Find out how animals are helping people in amazing ways. Contact: Angel Animals®, P. O. Box 26488, Minneapolis, Minnesota 55426. Tel: 888-925-3309. Fax: 612-925-4729. E-mail: angelanimals@aol.com. In Canada, contact the Ontario Society for the Prevention of Cruelty to Animals, 16640 Yonge Street, New Market, Ontario, L3Y 4V8. Tel: 905-898-7122. Fax: 905-853-8643. E-mail: info@ospca.on.ca.

Susan Kandell 1995

Healing and Helping

DARNELL GREEN

THE STRANGE TRUTH IS THAT WHEN I FIRST HAD the opportunity to meet my wife, I looked right past her. Kim
and I were in the same math class at the University of
Illinois in Chicago in 1985, but somehow I didn't notice her.
Now, loving her as I have, I can't imagine how I could have
passed her up. Luckily, though, we met through other circumstances. Once we started dating, I knew she was the
woman I wanted to be with forever.

That was surely my plan. But our plans and God's plans
aren't always the same. And when things get tough, it's hard to
just keep on going sometimes. Nevertheless, I know that's
what I have to do. That's what I learned from Kim. _____

Kim and I dated for quite a while before we got married. But we knew from the
beginning that we were a perfect match. We were both bright in school and shared
a lot of the same interests. And I was so attracted to her—both her physical beauty
and her maturity. This girl was so savvy.

We struggled together financially, and we definitely had days without any
money in our pockets. But we lived together while we were in school, and the
relationship grew stronger.

On July 23, 1989, we had a private marriage ceremony just between the two of us in our apartment. Kim had written up some vows, and we signed them that night. We promised to love, respect, and provide one another with the wisdom and knowledge needed to help us grow mentally, spiritually, physically, and financially. We promised to keep an open line of communication and talk out any disagreement that we would surely encounter throughout our lives together. We agreed to share in the rearing of our children, to teach them right from wrong, and to help them become better than us.

And as far as we were concerned, we were married. Then exactly one year later to the day, we went down to the justice of the peace and got married legally.

At that time, we both had jobs in Chicago. But when Kim became pregnant, she stopped working. We both believed that there's nothing better for a child than the love you can get from your mom, so she decided to stay home for a couple of years when Darius, our son, was born. While she was home, Kim taught herself how to run operating systems.

When Darius was two, Kim wanted to go back to work, and we let Darius stay with my mother in Michigan while Kim looked for a job. My mother was the only person we really trusted to watch him. Kim found a good job, we brought Darius back home, and we were happy. Life looked great.

Kim was a woman who always took good care of herself. Neither of us drank or smoked. When we met, I didn't eat pork or beef—a habit I picked up from my nine brothers who avoided the two for religious reasons—and Kim stopped eating those meats, too. We were both exercise enthusiasts and played a lot of tennis. All in all, we were both in great health.

But not too long after Kim went back to work, she started breaking out in a rash on her face at night. The doctors gave her a lot of different medications, but we just couldn't get rid of it. Eventually, they put her through all kinds of tests, looking for everything from diabetes to lupus to AIDS. But they never could find the problem. Finally, around January 1996, she changed jobs and stopped taking all medications, and the rash seemed to disappear. We thought Kim's health problems were behind us.

I had gone to Brazil for business around that time, and when I got back, Kim said she had found a lump in her breast. When I felt it, I knew she was right. The day before her thirtieth birthday, Kim went into the hospital for a biopsy. They told us immediately that she had cancer.

I was stunned and completely unprepared. How could this have happened—and happened so fast? Kim ate well, exercised, didn't drink or smoke, and had no history of cancer in her family. How could this have happened? We looked for answers everywhere.

After the biopsy, Kim had chemotherapy for three months, but none of the drugs did anything to shrink the tumor. After that, she had a radical mastectomy and radiation. Then a couple of months later, while she was still having radiation, she felt a lump under her arm on the opposite side of her body. The cancer had spread to the far side of her body—and into her brain as well.

In March 1997, while Kim was in the hospital, the doctor took me aside and said there was nothing more they could do for her. I went right back into the room and told Kim. We just didn't keep those kinds of things secret in our relationship. But I started to cry when I told her, and I couldn't stop crying. I thought I was never going to stop.

"Baby," she said, taking me in her arms, using her energy to comfort me despite being so sick. "Baby, you have to stop crying. If you don't, you'll make me cry, too. You can't carry on like this. You have to remember the good times we had and think about those. Darnell, I know it's hard—but you have to focus on the positives."

I felt so bad that Kim was the one comforting me. But the truth is she knew exactly what I needed to hear.

I took Kim home and tried to make her as comfortable as possible. Toward the end, she was in so much pain. I remember one night—a night that hurts even to remember—she was in so much pain that she couldn't lie in the bed. She asked me to hold her. She couldn't stand up, or sit down, or lie down. So I just held her in my arms.

That next day I went to my office and told them I didn't know when I would be back. I had to be with Kim. They were so wonderful. They told me just to do what I needed to do, and were even good enough to continue to pay me. That was a tremendous help.

I needed to be with Kim because I had to be there to make sure she had it her way. She said who could and could not come into the bedroom, depending on how she was feeling that day. And I slept on the floor next to the bed every night. She was my wife, and I would be there for her. Good, bad, or ugly—I would be there for her.

Kim passed on June 7, 1997. I got up to look at her that morning, and she was gone. I felt so much pain. She and Darius were the best things that had ever happened to me. But I know that the Lord has a mysterious way of operating. We never really know what He's going to do. It's all in His hands, all in His plans. That I knew for sure.

I got Darius up that morning and took him over to his grandmother's house. He was five years old, and I didn't want him to see his mother like that. Later that day, after everything had been cleaned up, I brought him home and told him that Mama was gone. I told him the whole truth—that the Lord had decided it was time for Mama to come home with Him, and Darius wasn't going to see her any more on this earth. I didn't pull any punches.

Even through my own pain that day, I hurt so much for that little boy. I still have my own parents—they're in their seventies and eighties—and I love them so much. I cannot even imagine how he must have felt. He cried, and I cried. I had done most of my crying alone when Kim was sick. But I didn't want to be afraid to cry in front of Darius just then. We both surely had something to cry about.

After Kim died—after the funeral and the burial—I tried to get on with things as best as I could. But really, I was bitter and I was angry. I would walk down the street and see someone smoking, and it would just drive me crazy.

"Lord," I would ask. "Why did you take Kim? She didn't smoke. She didn't drink. She ate right and she exercised. This person is standing here and smoking—alive as can be. But my boy's mother is gone. Why, Lord?"

I questioned and I questioned. For months, I was lonely and angry. I didn't know how I was going to go on with my life and raise Darius.

Then one day, thinking about Darius, I decided to watch a videotape Kim had left for him. She made the tape right before her mastectomy, when she realized the chemo hadn't worked. I guess she knew then that she might not be around to talk to Darius in person.

It was hard for me to watch the tape that day, and I still haven't shown it to Darius. I'll wait until I know the time is right for him. But I was so glad I watched it. It was wonderful—even through the pain—to see her face and hear her voice. She talked to Darius about her life and her family, and about how she and I met and married. I sat there with a big grin on my face, watching her talk about our relationship. Then there's another section, taped a few months later, that shows Kim reading to Darius while he sat on her lap.

After I saw that tape, I realized how proud Kim had been of us and our marriage. I knew I had to put the bitterness and anger behind me and move forward in my life. I had to do it for Darius, and I had to do it for myself. Kim was wise beyond her years, just like she showed when she wrote those beautiful wedding vows. And even after she passed, she was still teaching me.

One of the first things I did to try to set myself straight again was to go back to volunteering in the community with an organization I belong to, 100 Black Men of America. It's a group that brings together professional African American men to help out our youth. We have eighty chapters around the country now. We do mentoring and tutoring, but we also have prominent speakers talk to the children, host career days, work to physically clean up communities, and take the children to places of interest. We've taken our group to the Chicago Board of Options Exchange Trading floor and to the National Bar Association convention when it was held here.

I first heard about 100 Black Men when I was married, and the minute I told Kim about it, she told me to join. She thought it was a perfect match for me. I have always been so thankful for the childhood I had. I've had a strong support system all my life, but I know it's not like that for everyone. And I wanted to be able to help kids who didn't have that.

I've always loved helping children. I'm so tired of the negatives, the stereotypes and images we're always subjected to. There's no better way to get rid of that than to get your hands dirty. I got involved with the mentoring program—mentoring foster kids, too. I wanted to show them, by example, the real-world value of a good education.

Kim was the one who encouraged me to join in the first place. And, after watching the video she made, I felt like she was encouraging me to go back to life, get involved in the world again, help Darius, help these other children. She was telling me to get out there and make a difference—not to sit around and be bitter and angry. She knew that wouldn't do any good.

Going back to 100 Black Men helped me out tremendously. It helped me focus on someone else and their problems, instead of only on me and my problems.

And the mentoring keeps me grounded. Otherwise, I tend to forget where I came from. I forget what it takes to raise up a child who might not have a ready-made support system. We all need to get out there and do that work ourselves. We can't just take it for granted that someone else is going to do it. Kim's leaving me just reinforces the fact that you just can't take things for granted.

So now I'm committed to Darius, and I'm committed to helping as many other children as I can, too. That's what Kim wanted me to do. That's the message she sent me through that tape. She knew that was how I could make my contribution to others and heal my own wounds at the same time.

Share Darnell's dream for empowering our African American youth. Find out more about the eighty-two local chapters of 100 Black Men of America, Inc., providing our youth positive role models, educational assistance, and alternatives for achieving personal success. Contact: 100 Black Men of Chicago, Inc., 188 West Randolph, Suite 626, Chicago, Illinois 60601. Tel: 312-857-1997. Web site: **www.100blackmen.org.** In Canada, contact the YMCA of Wood Buffalo, 221 Tundra Drive, Fort McMurray, Alberta, T9H 4Z7. Tel: 403-790-9622. Fax: 403-743-4045.

Susan Kandell 1999

Giving Back

CARIDAD ASENSIO

I GREW UP IN CUBA. That's where I married and had my two children. Cuba is a beautiful land with wonderful people. But when Castro came in and took over, he turned my country upside down. Families were being torn apart. And I didn't want my children to grow up like that.

It was very hard to get my family to America. We weren't able to come all at once, and we had to live through the terrible pain of separation. It was so lonely. Some days I cried all the time. But once we were reunited in the United States, I knew I wanted to do something for the people here. And that's what I have been working on for the past thirty-eight years.

When my son, Manuel, was four years old, I knew it was time for him to leave Cuba. I saw lots of children as young as five being taken away from their parents, and I didn't want to lose my son. My sister and brother-in-law were getting ready to leave then, so I decided to send my son with them. I didn't know when I would see my little boy again, but I knew he would be safe with them, and he would not be safe if he stayed with me.

So I packed up Manuel's little clothes and we all went to the port. At the port, the people in charge told everyone to say good-bye to their loved ones. Then they put the men in one room and the women in another room. They made us take off all our clothes. And they searched us. I felt like I was losing my soul at that moment. I was so ashamed of myself, being naked in front of those people. I knew that in my whole life, I would never forget that.

From that moment on, I focused only on figuring out a way for the rest of my family to leave Cuba—and on when I would see my little Manuel again.

I worked and worked, and saved every single thing I could. Finally, someone told me a plane was leaving for Jamaica. I bought round-trip tickets for my mother, my two-year-old daughter, and myself, although I never intended to use the return-trip portion.

My husband stayed behind. He wasn't ready to leave yet, but he never told me not to go. He knew it was best.

When we got to Jamaica, we were hungry and had no place to stay. We had no money—the Cuban authorities took everything we had before we left. But thank God, there was a bank that helped us. They had a big empty house in the mountains, and they gave it to us and some other immigrants at a very low rent. There were forty of us living in that one house. But we were thankful to have a place to sleep. We lived there for a month, and our families sent us money. One day, we went to the American embassy and got good news. We would be able to go to the United States from Jamaica.

We arrived in Miami and stayed with an aunt for a few weeks. I couldn't find any work, so I bought a comb and a pair of scissors and went knocking on all the doors to see if anyone wanted a haircut. I didn't know how to cut hair, but guessed it was easy. Each person who needed a haircut paid me twenty or fifty cents. And at the end of the day, it was enough to buy some food.

After a few weeks, an agency aiding Cuban refugees sent us tickets to come to New York, where I had a sister and an aunt. When we arrived in New York, we had no winter clothes. We had never needed them before. But the people there gave us some warm clothes and a comb for our hair. I'll never forget the beautiful coats we were given. My daughter's was red, my mother's was black, and mine was green. Those coats lasted a long time—until we could afford to buy our own.

One cold day, while I was standing in line for some clothes, a man came in, took off his coat, put it on the table, and said, "Please, give this coat to someone who needs it more than me." And he left with just the suit he had on.

I cried when he did that. I thought, "Oh, my God. What a beautiful country. What a beautiful place where people do things like this for each other."

That was my first experience with the kindness and love the American people have. And I made my decision right then that I was going to do something one day to help these wonderful people who helped me and my family so much.

As soon as we got to New York, we started working, mostly in factories, and saved money so that Manuel could come to New York from Venezuela, where he was staying with my sister and brother-in-law.

No one can understand, unless they've been separated from someone they love, how much you suffer when you are away from your family. I never knew if I would see my son again. I cried every day on the subway on my way to work and every day on my way home. And I prayed day and night. I had faith in God. I knew that better times would come.

Finally I had enough money to send a ticket for my son. When Manuel arrived in the United States, it was such a happy day for me. It had been almost six months since I had seen him. I cried all night from happiness. I enrolled Manuel in school. By the end of the first month, he already knew English. I couldn't believe how fast he could learn.

A few months after Manuel's arrival, my husband came to New York, too. My whole family was together again. It was such a wonderful Christmas that year. We didn't have much, but we had love and we had each other.

My husband worked at IBM in New York for ten years, and then was transferred to Boca Raton, Florida. My son wanted to stay in New York to finish high school at the school he loved. But I said our family was going to stay together. So in 1971, we all moved to Boca Raton.

I got a job in the counselor's office at Boca Raton High School and loved working with the students there. Then one day, a woman I had become friendly with told me she had an even better job for me. It was as a community health worker for the Palm Beach County School Board, working with the Spanish community. I interviewed and got the job. And I worked there for seventeen years.

My own family did very well during the years I worked for the school board. My son graduated from high school and attended the Wharton School in Pennsylvania, one of the top colleges in the country. After that, he went to graduate school at Harvard. Now he owns his own business in New York, and my daughter has two wonderful daughters of her own now.

As my own children grew up and went on to lead these lives of their own, they needed less and less of my time. So I began to devote every single moment of my time to migrant workers and their families. They need so much. I wanted them to have better homes—better than the shacks they lived in. I wanted them to have the medical attention they needed. And I wanted them to have a good education for their children.

These hard-working people come to America from Mexico, El Salvador, Honduras, Nicaragua, and Guatemala. They work every day from sunrise to sunset in the fields to bring food to the table for Americans, who have so much. And they deserve a better life.

In 1989, with the help of some of my friends, I started an organization called the Migrant Association of South Florida. We are a nonprofit organization dedicated to helping migrant children. This was the job that God meant for me to do. I know that. God was just directing my life. I don't know how He knows the direction my life should take, but He does.

The first thing I wanted to do was improve migrants' living conditions. So we found people willing to donate old mobile homes or sell them to us at a good price. Then we painted each trailer, cleaned it up, and loaned it to a family. If the family took good care of it for one year, we deeded the trailer to them.

Every time I was able to put a family in a mobile home, I felt wonderful. That's because I know firsthand what it means to be grateful to have electricity and running water and a hot shower.

After we got the mobile-home program started—we have provided homes for 165 families—I decided to open a medical clinic for children. People told me I would never get doctors and nurses to volunteer their time and that the migrant families wouldn't come. But I just kept working.

In 1992, the day before Hurricane Andrew struck, we opened the Caridad Health Clinic in a small trailer. We had more than 1,000 phone calls from people wanting to volunteer their time—doctors, nurses, dentists. And we had more than 300 people waiting to get inside the day it opened. It was such a wonderful day. There was so much love in there. You could look in the faces of those volunteers and just cry from happiness.

After that clinic opened, I had a dream to build a bigger clinic—one that could meet all the needs of the migrant community. When people heard about our work, some wealthy people came forward and donated money. It is unbelievable how generous people have been. We were able to buy a piece of land and build a clinic.

In November 1997, we opened the Caridad Health Clinic in the Count and Countess de Hoernle Pavilion on the Caridad Health Campus. We have twelve exam rooms, an X-ray machine, and a pharmacy. We have more than 170 medical volunteers and 300 other volunteers. We treat about 5,000 patients a year now. More and more people knock on our door every day. And when they do, we don't ask any questions. We just open our arms and our hearts to greet them.

But we do make sure that everyone who uses the clinic gives a small donation. I don't care if it's just a couple of coins. People feel better about themselves, they have better self-esteem, when they pay for something. When my family arrived in this country, we went to work immediately. No one thought about welfare or food stamps. "I help you because you help yourself," I tell migrant workers. And for every service they use, they must give a donation back.

The next thing I want to do is build an educational building where we can help children with their homework, with their reading and writing. I'm trying to get the money together for that now.

I hope God gives me the strength to see that project finished. That will complete my life. I want to give to this country so much. I want to give everything.

Help improve conditions for migrant farm workers in South Florida and/or in your region. Contact: Migrant Association of South Florida, 8645 West Boynton Beach Boulevard, Boynton Beach, Florida 33437. Tel: 561-737-6336. Fax: 561-737-9232.

CHAPTER 12

Susan Kandell 1999

To Have and to Hug

AMANDA PERLYN

WHEN I WAS IN FIRST GRADE, I had an experience that changed my life. Actually, it ended up changing my whole family's life. And through our efforts, it's continued to change many other people's lives, too.

I know a lot of people have deep experiences when they're much older. But for me, I was seven. I will never forget the power of the lesson I learned that year, and I'm thankful it came into my life when I was so young. Now I'm seventeen, and I have come to understand that no matter how old you are, you can learn how to make a difference in the life of someone less fortunate than yourself. _____

My first-grade teacher was Dr. Margaurite Malko at Pine Crest Preparatory School in Ft. Lauderdale, Florida. When I learned that I was in her class, I was a little bit scared. I thought she was a medical doctor, and that we might all have to line up for shots on the first day of school. But before we could even ask any questions, she told us right away not to worry. She said she had a doctorate in education and wasn't going to be giving anybody any shots.

That was a good example of how Dr. Malko handled everything the whole school year. She seemed to anticipate our concerns, our issues, our problems. She felt more like a mom than a teacher. When you were in her class, she cared about you so much. And because of how wonderful she was, all the kids just loved her back. She made even the simplest activities so warm and wonderful.

Then one day, Dr. Malko told our class that there was something she needed to share with us. She told us that her daughter, Elena, was sick. She said there might be days when Elena would need her and she wouldn't be in school but that there would be another teacher in her place.

Being first graders, we all figured Elena must have a cold or the flu. But Dr. Malko told us it was something different, and that she would explain it to us.

A few days later Elena came to school to visit our class. Elena, who was twenty-seven then, was wearing a hat. She sat down and took off her hat—she was bald. We were all amazed. We had never seen a bald woman before. That's when Dr. Malko explained about Elena's illness and about chemotherapy.

Elena came to school from time to time after that, and we all loved visiting with her. But I don't think we ever completely understood how really sick she was because she always smiled and looked happy. After a while, though, Elena stopped coming to visit, and we started having a substitute more and more often.

On the days Dr. Malko was at school, she always did her best to act cheery and normal. But sometimes I would catch a glimpse of her face when she didn't think anyone was looking, and I could see how worried she was. I hated seeing her that way. She was everything to me, and it hurt me so badly inside to know she was so sad.

One day, I overheard Dr. Malko talking to another teacher about Elena. Dr. Malko told her that Elena was still receiving treatment. Dr. Malko's husband had died from cancer many years ago. With only one income, it was difficult for her to pay for Elena's medical expenses. I was concerned about how Elena would get treatment if Dr. Malko didn't have the money.

When I came home from school that day and told my parents what I had heard, I was close to tears. "What can we do to help Dr. Malko?" I asked. "I have to figure out some way to help her."

After talking it over, we decided we would make and sell Christmas ornaments to raise money for Elena's bills. My parents and my brothers, Chad and Eric, worked with me. We took the bark from palm trees and made them into reindeer faces. I went around my neighborhood door to door selling them for $10 each.

I raised $1,000 and brought a box full of money to school. When I handed that pile of cash to Dr. Malko, I felt like the biggest person on earth. Then she said something to me that I will never forget. "When children help others, they are like angels with invisible halos on their heads."

When I saw her tears of happiness, my life was changed. I understood then that I really had the ability to make a difference in someone's life, even though I was only seven years old. I knew right then I was committed to continuing to make a difference for people who needed help.

Shortly afterward, Elena died. All of us students were so sad. I went to the funeral with my parents and many of my classmates. After the funeral, we went back to Dr. Malko's house. Dr. Malko was so strong and courageous. I remember her hugging all of us and assuring us that she would be OK.

The next year, I kept going back to visit Dr. Malko in her classroom. She wasn't my teacher anymore, but I still loved her so much and thought about her all the time. That year around Christmas, my mom and I saw an announcement about an essay contest. The contest was to write an essay about someone you wish could be with you for the holidays. The winner would receive an airplane ticket to visit the person they wrote about.

"I could write this essay for Dr. Malko," I said to my mom. "She will be alone for the holidays if she doesn't visit her son, Michael, in Idaho. Without a free ticket, she won't be able to do that."

I didn't think I could win a contest that was supposed to be for adults. But I thought I'd give it a try. I wrote about Elena and all that Dr. Malko had been through. And then I added, "The other day, I had a Chinese fortune cookie. It said, 'An emptiness soon will be filled.' Now I want to give my fortune to someone else."

The people who sponsored the contest called me at school to say that I had won! Dr. Malko was overjoyed. She insisted on calling the local television station because she said, "The world should know about a child who cares." Her words and actions reinforced that caring for others was a special act of kindness. But I was just so happy that she got the free plane ticket and went to Idaho to spend Christmas with her son.

Not too long after that, my mother met someone who works with children who have to testify in court against their parents in cases of physical or sexual abuse. I felt so sorry for those children. I knew how much my family meant to me, and I wished they had a family like mine. Since I couldn't give them that kind of family love, I thought it would be great if they each had a teddy bear to give them a hug—something warm and cuddly they could take into the courtroom with them.

So in fourth grade, I started an organization called "To Have and to Hug." I designed a logo and my dad got stationery printed. I wrote a letter explaining what I wanted to do. Then I went door to door through the malls, meeting with store managers; usually, they would give me a few stuffed animals. As the project grew,

I started writing letters to toy manufacturers, and some of them sent boxes and boxes of teddy bears.

One of the organizations I work with, Children's Home Society, always has a big party for kids at Easter, so we thought that would be a good time to give out the bears. It turned out there were 100 children, and I had bears for them all. I've done that project now for eight years in a row. Every year, I pray we'll have fewer and fewer children—fewer children who have been through the pain of abuse. But so far, I've distributed about 2,500 bears.

The really exciting thing is that my whole family has become involved in "To Have and to Hug," and they've started their own projects, too—just from seeing that one person really can make a difference. My oldest brother, Chad, started Doc Adopt, an organization that matches doctors and dentists with underprivileged kids who need care.

My other brother, Eric, called the Children's Home Society to ask what else the kids there needed. It turns out they really needed shoes. So he started an organization called "Stepp'n Up." Just like me, Eric went mall to mall to talk to the store managers to collect shoes. And the program just grew like crazy. When Eric left for college, I started working on this project, too.

We've given out about 10,000 pairs of shoes. We have warehouse space now to house all the teddy bears and shoes. We've also written a manual to show other kids how to start these programs in their own towns. The manual is available to anyone, and we send it to people all over the country.

It's really fun to give things out to these kids and to see the excitement and pride on their faces. But it wouldn't really mean so much if you didn't have a chance to hear their stories. That's when I really feel the pain of their situation.

I remember one time I wanted to give a teddy bear to a little girl. She looked so sad when I walked up to her. But the minute I put the teddy bear in her arms, she smiled and gave me a big hug. Then I found out that just a week earlier, she had been found home alone—naked and in a cage.

These are just such sick, terrible, sad stories. But the most incredible thing to me is that I have the power to make this child smile—this child who has been put through so much terror and trauma. I do one little thing—collect a bear and give it to her—and it means so, so much to her.

I work hard in school, and I work hard on my projects. I'm not missing any of the other things that kids do. Helping others doesn't take away from your life—it adds to it, and I wouldn't trade it for anything in the world.

I've never really talked about my projects all that much at school. It's just something I do for myself, at nights or on weekends with my family. But some of my friends do know about it. Some of them help out every now and then. And others come up and say, "Amanda, why are you wasting your time? What are you doing all this for anyway?"

For me, the answer to that question came from my experience with Dr. Malko. If I hadn't felt the pain of someone I loved so much, I might not be doing this today.

My family was an average, everyday family who participated in standard giving before we met Dr. Malko and Elena. My parents gave money to charities, we donated clothing, we collected cans for food drives, we volunteered when needed. But when we made those reindeer faces, we realized the impact we could have on someone else's life.

Now both of my brothers, my parents, and I understand how important it is to help others. And we want to share what we have learned. My parents counsel other families about how to get involved in meaningful community service work, work that builds on each family's unique interests and talents.

I've come to see that when you go out there in the world and help people, you're really helping yourself, too. When you're out there giving and seeing how happy you can make another person, you can't stop the great feeling that comes over you. If you are a teenager with a problem—even a really serious problem—I say don't sit in your room continuing to feel badly. Get out there and help someone—someone whose pain is greater than your own. You will realize a change in your own life in the process.

Like Amanda, you can experience the joy of giving at any age. Start your own project with a step-by-step instruction manual, and/or find out how you can help an existing Stepp'n Up. Contact: Heart of America Foundation, c/o Steppin' Up, 201 Massachusetts Avenue NE, Suite CE, Washington D.C. 20002. Tel: 202-546-3256. Fax: 202-546-3257. E-mail: heartofamerica@erols.com. Web site: **www.heartofamerica.org.**

Susan Kandell 1998

Lifeline to Freedom

BARBARA PITTMAN

I MARRIED THE ONLY BOY I HAD EVER DATED, straight out of high school. I was naive, foolish, and grateful to have found what I assumed to be love. But I quickly realized I had been mistaken ever to have thought that man loved me.

That mistake almost cost me my life. But through the grace of God, I eventually escaped that prison of violence. It will probably take me the rest of my life to heal the wounds that were inflicted on me. But I'm working on it. I'm working on it by doing everything I possibly can to make sure no other woman ever has to walk in my footsteps. And I'll just keep working on it. ————————————————————————

In 1966, I was a high school senior in Philadelphia. I was overweight, shy, and didn't have many friends. My parents had been very strict about dating. So when my mother met a stockboy at her office, a boy she thought was nice, she asked him over to our house to meet me.

When I first met Roger, I thought he was nice, too. He paid attention to me and seemed to be a real gentleman, so we started dating. Roger took me to the prom that year. There I was—Barbara—dancing at the prom! I felt so lucky.

Roger and I were married the summer after I graduated and immediately moved to Key West, Florida. Roger had a stressful job on a naval base and worked long hours. Although I wanted to get a job, Roger wouldn't allow it.

So I was home alone all day, away from family and friends. All I had was the list of chores Roger left for me to do every day. He insisted that I clean the house in a very specific way for hours each day. And if he came home to find any chore not done just the way he had wanted it, he would yell and scream, barking out orders and calling me names. If I turned to walk away while he was still talking, he would grab my arm so hard that his hand would leave a bruise.

That's when the fights started—almost immediately after we were married.

I tried to talk to my mother about it. But my mother had worked all her life, and all she could think about was how lucky I was that I didn't have to work. When I told her I felt trapped and frightened, she said it really wasn't all that much for a man to ask his wife to pull her weight and take care of the chores. My husband was putting food on the table and clothes on my back, and he had a right to have a clean house, didn't he? After all, what else did I really have to do?

I knew that it was my job to keep the house clean. And that was fine. But it was the way Roger ordered me around and the way he spoke to me that frightened me—the violence in his anger, the threats, my confusion and fear. And the knowledge that I had no one to turn to.

We had been married for two years when Roger hit me for the first time. He had just come back from serving thirteen months in Vietnam, and I had moved back in with my parents during that time. Two days after he returned, I said I wanted to go out to dinner to celebrate his homecoming. He said he wanted me to cook dinner. When I opened my mouth to discuss it with him, he slapped me across the face. Then he asked me why I had made him do that.

Roger blamed his behavior on me from the beginning. And I believed him. I thought I could change his behavior if I just tried harder to please him. If I could just scrub the floor faster, or remember when he did and did not want me to use wax. If I could just do things right, he might stop the slapping and punching and kicking.

Not too long after he came back from Vietnam, we moved into a house two doors down from my parents in Philadelphia, and I became pregnant with my first child. I wanted that baby so badly. I thought about how wonderful it would be to have someone to love—and someone who loved me. I thought Roger might change, too, when he had a baby to love. Maybe those weren't the best reasons to want a baby, but I loved that child so much.

But that baby was the first of my three children who died before they had a chance to be born.

My first baby died because I couldn't scrub the floor fast enough. I wasn't feeling so well from my pregnancy and was slowing down a bit. One day, Roger saw me scrubbing the kitchen floor and said I was working too slowly. He came over and started kicking me in the stomach. And that baby was stillborn.

When I got pregnant again, I hoped that things would be different this time. Instead, Roger pushed me down a flight of steps in my ninth month. And that baby was stillborn, also. I lost my third baby because Roger made a U-turn in the middle of a busy street while we were in the car in my ninth month. Roger wasn't hurt, but I went through the windshield. And my third baby died.

When I became pregnant for the fourth time, Roger stopped the physical abuse for a while. I really don't know why. Maybe he thought people were becoming suspicious of me losing all these children. The hospital probably suspected what I had been through, but there were no laws to protect women in those days. Whatever the reason, the abuse stopped. And I thankfully gave birth to Steven, a beautiful, healthy son, in 1972.

When Steven was about four months old, the physical violence started again. And it didn't stop. Both of my next two children—Rachel and Andrew—were born premature because of the physical abuse I suffered. Andrew had to stay in the hospital for months because he was so tiny, and he had medical problems throughout his childhood and adolescence.

When Andrew was born, Roger moved us out to the suburbs, away from family. And he became even more controlling. He never allowed me out of the house, not even to take the children to school or to buy groceries. He did everything— just to keep me locked up, just to be able to control me every minute. So by that time, I was living in a prison.

I was grateful that Roger never turned his violence against the children. But because I was suffering from constant physical abuse, I could hardly take care of my kids— especially Andrew who was so sick. On top of that, I knew my children had to listen to the slapping, the punching, the screaming. One day, when Andrew was one and a half, I just couldn't stand it any more.

I made the first of four attempted escapes. Each time, Roger found us after only a few days. And each time, I came back when he threatened to go to court and take my children away from me.

It's hard to describe how bad the abuse became during those years. He beat me, kicked me, knocked my teeth out, burned me with cigarettes, pushed me through a window, slashed me with a razor, raped me with a gun held to my head, and cut me inside and out with glass. Each time he attacked me, I thought I just couldn't live through it one more time. But I did—for my children.

By 1981, after fifteen years of abuse, I was feeling so desperate, I didn't know what to do. I turned to my mother, but, unbelievably, she still thought I was making up the abuse. As a last resort, I turned to God.

I can't say that I was real happy with God right about then. Some days, I wasn't even sure God existed. I felt that He had been punishing me for years—and I didn't know why. But even with my doubts and fears, I turned to God. I was desperate.

Every night, I cried and I bargained with God: "Lord, if You help me, if You help me and my children get out of this horrible situation, I will dedicate my life to helping other people. I will do everything I can to help other women who have been through this."

Just a few weeks after I began that prayer, I finally escaped from Roger for good. Roger's younger brother had just committed suicide, and I was counting on the fact that Roger was too distraught to come looking for me. I left while Roger was at the funeral.

The kids and I left with the clothes on our backs and moved back to Philadelphia. It was very scary. Roger knew where we were. He knew where the children's school was. He stalked us for years. He knew everything I did. But he never tried to get me back.

About two years after the children and I left, I started going to college. I was on welfare, raising the kids, going to school, and trying to make a stable home for them. It was never easy. But it was the beginning of a life. And I graduated from college in three years, with a specialty in mental health.

It was at school that I first felt a sense of support coming from another human being. In one of my classes, there was a woman I started becoming friendly with. Somehow I just knew she had also been abused. We didn't talk about it at first, but battered women often have a common bond they can just sense. Eventually, we started talking about our lives, and the stories of abuse came out. Finally, I had someone I could relate to, someone who believed me, someone who understood. And that gave me a tremendous sense of hope.

All the time I was in school, working so hard to try to put my life back together, I never forgot my bargain with God. And so I started working to help battered women as soon as I could.

Since 1985, even before I finished school, I have been working with organizations that support and advocate for victims of domestic violence—Women Against Abuse, Women in Transition, and the National Coalition Against Domestic Violence.

I have counseled women, spoken out on TV and radio, taught violence-prevention workshops at high schools and colleges, worked as a hotline counselor, and testified before Congress about the problem of domestic violence. I have facilitated support groups for abused women who are now in prison, being punished for the fact that they physically fought back against their attackers. And I'm currently working as program coordinator for Working Wardrobe, an organization that provides nice clothes for job interviews at no charge to disadvantaged women who are in job-training programs.

I've also created programs myself when I've seen a need that wasn't being addressed. Along with my wonderful husband Scot Pittman—a man of tremendous patience, who showed me for the first time in my life what it really means to love and cherish someone—I have created the Street Clothes Project in Philadelphia. Working Wardrobe provides clothes for those in training programs, but the need goes way beyond that. Street Clothes provides clothing and personal care items at no charge to men and women who are moving from a life of dependence to independence, and we also provide clothes for their children.

When women come in to Street Clothes, they almost always walk with their head down and eyes on the floor. Their hair and clothes are usually dirty, and their image of themselves is dirty, too. But as they start trying on professional clothes—

clothes that would be part of the working world—they begin to stand taller and stronger. I can just watch them and know they are allowing themselves to imagine a good future for the very first time—the possibility of things going right, the possibility of feeling good about themselves.

What I really see when I help these women is hope. And that is what my work is all about.

Many of the adults who come into Street Clothes are transitioning from life in prison to life outside, or from drug or alcohol rehab to a new life of responsibility. And many of our women and children are working to build new lives after escaping from domestic violence.

Some people have commented that they thought it was strange for me to be working with a program that helps men as well as women, after what I've been through. But I don't see anything strange about it. I've learned I can't have the attitude that all men are bad. There are men out there who are good people, but who find themselves in bad situations. And just like I needed help, sometimes they just need a little help, too. It took me a long time to be able to trust men. But I have learned to judge people one at a time.

Some days, this work is not easy. Some days, I can't seem to get away from my own terrifying memories, because I spend so much time listening to the painful stories of other abused women. When I see a woman come in with a black eye or a bruise or a cut, it breaks my heart. And the closer a woman's story is to my own, the harder it is for me emotionally. Sometimes I do get bitter.

But when it hurts me to hear these women's stories—or to talk about the details of my own life one more time—I think about the fact that if I can save one life by speaking out about this violence over and over, then it's worth every bit of the painful feelings I go through.

My dream for the future is to build a shelter for battered women. And when I build this shelter, that will fulfill the final part of my promise to God. It's a big job, I know. But by working to help other women, my life makes sense. And it's the only way I can continue to heal—by helping others.

Women who need assistance can call any time. If you wish to donate and/or start your own project, contact: Street Clothes Project, P. O. Box 52208, Philadelphia, Pennsylvania 19115. Tel: 214-464-3955. Fax: 215-464-0843. E-mail: barb7849@aol.com. In Canada, contact The Barbra Schlifer Commemorative Clinic, 489 College Street, Suite 503, Toronto, Ontario, M6G 1A5. Tel: 416-323-9149. Fax: 416-323-9107. E-mail: bscc@web.net.

CHAPTER 14

Bill Thomas and family

Warren Bunn 1997

Back to the Garden

WILLIAM H. THOMAS, M.D.

I N MY FOUR YEARS AT HARVARD MEDICAL SCHOOL, I never stepped foot inside a nursing home. The way I saw it, I was destined for better places and greater things than taking care of old people day after day. So I trained to be an emergency room doctor, and I enjoyed the variety and excitement of ER care, although I missed the ability to develop long-term relationships with my patients. Then one day, the administrator of a nursing home asked me to consider becoming the home's doctor. I said I wasn't interested. But the administrator was persistent—very persistent—and I eventually took the job. I couldn't have known at that time that working at this nursing home would be most important job of my life. _____

Working at the nursing home, I saw too much emphasis on treatment and too little emphasis on care for the individual. I would provide medical care for my patients, but I didn't seem to be really helping them. At first, I didn't understand what the problem was. But after a while, I realized that residents were receiving treatment for congestive heart failure, for example, while their real suffering—

from loneliness, helplessness, and boredom—was left untreated. When I looked through my medical books and journals to find treatment for those very real problems, I found that none of those topics was even addressed.

I began to realize that we think of older people as nothing more than their bodies—bodies that break down and need to be repaired with medicine and surgery. What's missing is the view of "elderhood" as a precious time of teaching and wisdom that can only be gained by traveling far down life's path. I realized we need to look at elders not as broken-down human beings, but as wise souls.

With that concept of aging in mind, I considered our residents' problems in a new light. I asked myself how we would treat their primary problems of loneliness, helplessness, and boredom if they were younger people. And the answers became clear: To combat loneliness, we would provide them with companionship. To overcome helplessness, we would give them an opportunity to give to others. To alleviate boredom, we would add spontaneity and variety to their lives.

All of these things were missing in the nursing home.

To rectify this situation, I wrote a grant proposal, which was funded by the New York State Department of Health, and developed a plan I called the Eden Alternative™. We brought animals, plants, children, fun, spontaneity, and laughter into this home. And when looking for someone to help me manage the project, I placed this ad in the newspaper: "If you love plants, animals, and children, this job is for you."

The woman who responded to that ad is now my wife, Jude. She still laughs remembering that she called about the ad only because she thought something was wrong with it. She was sure two ads had mistakenly been combined. Her father had recently died in a nursing home under horrible conditions, and she felt sure that plants, animals, and children just couldn't belong in an ad about a nursing home. In fact, after losing her father, Jude had vowed to never step foot in another nursing home. Luckily, though, her wonderful sense of intrigue motivated her to call us. And after coming out and seeing a nursing home filled with birds, dogs, children, live plants, and residents whose spirits were being cared for—the first Eden model—she changed her mind. Jude became the Eden Alternative™ coordinator. Two years later we married.

In June 1994, our first little girl, Haleigh Jane, was born. We were ecstatic. My two sons from a previous marriage, Zachary and Virgil, lived with us, and now we also had a child of our own. We were so happy with our beautiful family.

But before too many days had passed, that happiness turned to worry. Although Jude nursed her, Haleigh kept losing weight. We tried a supplement, but she still lost weight. Jude's instincts told her this was more than just a nursing problem—possibly some type of intestinal blockage—and she took Haleigh to the pediatrician. But the news we received that day was worse than anything we had imagined. After a physical exam and brain wave test, the doctor told Jude that Haleigh had Idiopathic Infantile Encephalopathy, a severe neurological disorder.

Jude called me immediately, and together we talked with the doctor. He told us our precious little girl would never see, never walk, never talk.

We were so shocked and grief-stricken we could barely take in what the doctor was telling us. Our hearts broke in that office, and, in some ways, we have never really been the same since. "How could this happen?" we asked ourselves a hundred times that day.

"How could this happen to such a beautiful, innocent child? Why? Why? Why?"

We took Haleigh to the best pediatric neurologists in the world. Every doctor we saw confirmed our own pediatrician's diagnosis and prognosis. They called Haleigh's condition a one-in-a-million case of bad luck. It was just a fluke, they said. Not genetic, just a fluke.

As we faced the reality of our future, we were determined to make life as beautiful for Haleigh as possible. By this time, Jude and I were committed to introducing the Eden Alternative™ to nursing homes all over the world, and we took Haleigh with us wherever we went. She accompanied us to England, Scotland, and all over the United States. We loved her and held her and gave her the security of our presence. We were a team. And, with the older boys, we loved the joy of being a family.

Before long, we decided we wanted another child. After extensive genetic counseling and testing, the doctors reaffirmed that Haleigh's disease was not genetic and that we should continue with our plans to have more children.

And so little Hannah was born on February 3, 1997.

Within twenty-four hours of Hannah's birth, Jude saw the baby's first seizure. When Jude shared her fears with family and friends, everyone assured her she was frightened for no reason. The baby had probably just stretched or shuddered a bit, and Jude had imagined it was a seizure. Nevertheless, we took Hannah to a pediatric neurologist. When he told us her tests were all normal, we went out to dinner to celebrate our relief.

But within weeks, Hannah started having seizures. We took her back to the doctor, and this time, her tests were abnormal. Even the doctor was devastated. None of us wanted to face the truth: Neither of our beautiful, precious daughters will ever see, talk, or walk.

The news about Hannah tore my wife's heart apart. And seeing her in that pain almost destroyed me. There is no deeper pain than knowing our children will never have lives of their own. But I knew I needed to be strong for Jude and the girls, so I tried to keep my emotions in check.

Eventually—and predictably—I broke down, too. No one can keep so much pain inside forever. At the time, I had gone from our home in Sherburne, New

York, to Texas to work with a nursing home that was adopting the Eden Alternative™, and I was doing a public reading from my book *Open Hearts, Open Minds*. The book is a work of fiction based on the principles of the Eden Alternative™. In the novel, Jude and I are transported to a land where people understand the value of building a society around the needs and capacities of the Elders. Haleigh and Hannah are the names of two wise teachers in the book. And in this work of fiction, we can hear their voices—something we will never experience in our real lives.

So here I was reading from the book in front of 250 people. I was reading a section in which a character named Judy gets bitten by a spider. All of a sudden I started to cry, and I just could not stop.

Through my tears, I finally said to my audience, "This is not about my Judy. I know she is home and she's safe and she has not been bitten by a spider. It's really about my girls and the fact that we go from day to day just never knowing how long we're going to have them." And with that, a woman from the back of the room—a woman I had never met before—came up and put her arms around me. Others followed and formed a big circle around me.

When I called home to tell Jude about it, I told her it hadn't been very professional of me to cry like that in public. Through her own tears, she said, "Bill Thomas, it was so very *human* of you."

Our girls now have full-time nursing care at home. And the truth is that we are not only promoting the Eden Alternative™ in our professional lives, we are living the Eden Alternative™ at home. We try to give our girls every opportunity for stimulation and human contact. Our nurses have become an extension of our family. And with their help, the girls have been able to avoid spending much time in the hospital.

Haleigh and Hannah are so easy to love. They coo, and Haleigh Jane has the most incredible smile you have ever seen. I love to carry her from her toes and wrestle with her. And she loves that closeness, too. She has this wonderful little laugh that lets me know she is happy.

I wish things were different. I would do anything in the world to make my girls well. But in a very profound sense, they are my most important teachers just exactly the way they are. Haleigh and Hannah can teach me things no one else can. And I'm not sure I even understand how that happens myself. We are so grateful for the path our lives took before the girls were born.

We are so grateful to have developed and seen the Eden Alternative™ in action before we needed it to be a part of our own lives.

We know now that working to bring the Eden Alternative™ to our elders all over the world has allowed us to learn how to give our own girls the most wonderful life possible. We have dogs, birds, and goats at our home for their companionship and ours. Our nurses never wear uniforms, and, although we do have some necessary medical equipment, our home looks like a home. We have avoided the institutional look that so many nursing homes reflect. The girls are always stimulated. And they are so happy because they know they are loved.

We have seen the benefits of the Eden Alternative™ in our own home, and we have seen its benefits in the lives of elders all over the world. Families look forward to visiting their loved ones in "Edenized" nursing homes because they know they'll have a pleasant visit. Instead of being depressed and bored—and boring to their visitors—residents talk about what the bird did today or what the dogs did or what the residents have been harvesting in the garden. We see children and grandchildren coming into the nursing homes to visit a lot more than they used to. One nursing home administrator calls this the "parking lot" theory. Parking lots are full on weekends at the nursing homes that have been Edenized. That may not be the most scientific way to judge success, but it says a lot to me.

Even more telling are the stories I hear daily. One resident, Mr. Paul, lost his wife of sixty years. Not too long after her death, he was in an accident and was brought to a nursing home to recuperate. He was frail and depressed and stayed in bed all the time.

Then one day, Ginger, one of the dogs at the home, found his way into Mr. Paul's room. The next day, one of the staff saw Mr. Paul raising himself up in bed to pet Ginger and scratch the dog's ears. Soon they found Mr. Paul sitting on the edge of the bed. He told the staff someone needed to walk Ginger, and he'd be glad to do it. From that day on, he was at the door at 4 P.M. every day, dressed and ready to walk Ginger. He regained his strength and good spirits. Mr. Paul returned to his own home within six months.

I hear about residents reading stories to children, residents watering and pruning the plants. Pharmacy bills have been cut in half at some Edenized facilities, and infection rates and mortality have been reduced. These remarkable improvements continue to show us that giving is as important as receiving. When someone is needed, they have a reason to live.

Today we have eighteen regional coordinators who are training nursing home staff all over the country. We have about 1,500 trained associates around the country and more than 300 nursing homes using the Eden Alternative™. As a family we are taking a bus tour around the country and making the Eden Alternative™ available to all who are willing to embrace it.

We have learned so much about the power of love from our wonderful girls. And we believe others can learn from them, too. The idea that human suffering can be instructive is something we need to take a hard look at. By learning the lessons that suffering can teach us, we can make the world around us a better place. The really important, deep, hard lessons are there, in the suffering. I know that no sane person chooses to learn those lessons or chooses a path that brings suffering into his or her life. But fate brought us Haleigh and Hannah, two beautiful girls who are total love. Fate also brought me my wonderful wife, Jude, who lives each day with grace and dignity. I feel it is my obligation to study the lessons well that Haleigh and Hannah have brought us, and use them to help as many people as possible live as fully as possible.

Become a part of the Eden Alternative™. Share Dr. Thomas' vision of creating human habitats filled with companionship, spontaneity, laughter, and love by contacting: The Eden Alternative™, 742 Turnpike Road, Sherburne, New York 13460. Tel: 607-674-5232. Fax: 607-674-6723. Web site: **www.edenalt.com.** In Canada, contact The Ontario Coalition of Senior Citizens' Organizations, 3101 Bathurst Street, Suite 500, Toronto, Ontario, M6A 2A6. Tel: 416-785-8570. Fax: 416-785-7361. E-mail: OCSCO@web.net.

The 9,000 Things

W MITCHELL

I LIVE IN A WHEELCHAIR THESE DAYS. At one time, this chair felt like my prison. It confined me, kept me from going where I wanted to go. My body used to be a prison, too. The stubs of my fingers, my burned skin—my outward appearance used to be a prison that kept me confined to the world inside myself.

But now, my body and my wheelchair form the platform that supports me. They are the vehicles that have helped me grow beyond myself and travel the world, helping others. I've learned that our bodies are just a thin veneer that can never hide the remarkable gifts that live inside each and every one of us. And I've also learned that even if you can't do some of the things you used to do, there are always 9,000 things you *can* do. _____

I didn't always have these short fingers and this wheelchair. In fact, as a young man, I worked as a gripman on the San Francisco cable cars. I can't think of too many more physically challenging jobs, and I absolutely loved it. I was on top of the world. I saw myself as a San Francisco bohemian, a man who could do anything. Yes, I had a few too many girlfriends and a bad temper. But I was one happy guy. I just wanted two things out of life at that point—a motorcycle and a pilot's license—and I was working to get them both.

In July 1971, I bought a brand new motorcycle. It was huge and powerful, and I loved it. The day after I bought it, I drove myself to the airfield and took my first solo flight.

It's hard to describe the emotional sensation you get from flying an airplane by yourself. You are the master of your fate, soaring, just soaring, with such a sense of both freedom and responsibility. I will never forget it.

When I left the airfield after my flight that day, I drove my motorcycle back to San Francisco—and my life was changed forever. A laundry truck ran a stop sign, smashing my motorcycle and knocking me to the ground. The force of the accident knocked the cap off the motorcycle's gas tank, spilling gasoline all over me. And the heat of the motorcycle engine ignited it.

When I regained consciousness two weeks later, and the doctors told me I would live, I wondered why I should bother. My life as I knew it was over. Sixty-five percent of my body was horribly burned, including my face and my fingers. I was in excruciating, unbelievable agony, and the procedures medical personnel performed on me were never-ending. They worked on me twenty-four hours a day—stretching, squeezing, bandaging, poking, and grafting skin.

What future could there possibly be for me?

But even in the middle of such pain, there were people who came forward to help, people whose prayers, love, and care helped me believe in the possibility of life.

There was Joe Williams, a maintenance man at the hospital. Sometimes even when Joe wasn't working on my floor, he would come up and stick his head in my room.

"Hey, Mitchell, how you doin', man? Hang in there," he would say. "You're gonna make it man!" I will never forget Joe's words of comfort and support. They helped me believe that pain was inevitable, but suffering was optional.

There was June Fulbright, one of my nurses. About a month after the accident, I quietly told June that I was sure I had died, that I had actually not survived the accident. It was the only view of my life that made sense at that time.

June responded by proving to me that I was alive. She put me in a wheelchair and took me outside the hospital for the first time. She forced me to believe in the trees, the sunlight, the city, the people. She was right. I was definitely alive, and I am eternally grateful to her for forcing me to see that.

A philosophy I had been studying before the accident also played a big role in my life at that time, and ever since. This philosophy is called Morehouse, and its three basic principles can be boiled down to this: First, accept yourself as you are. Second, there is no absolute relationship between situation and response—you are free to choose how to respond to any given situation. For example, money does not necessarily bring happiness. Conversely, and more important to my situation at the time, physical pain does not necessarily bring emotional disaster. And third, you are responsible for your life.

During my recovery, I focused as best as I could on these principles. It wasn't easy, and some days it took a tremendous effort, but I made a conscious decision to not see my accident as the end of my life.

For example, when I first realized that my fingers had been all but amputated in surgery to removed the burned skin—and all the doctors and nurses in the room expected me to become hysterical—I calmly told them I thought this would seriously mess up my pool game.

I used to have fingers. Now I don't. Those were the facts that day, and they're the facts now. The way in which I interpret those facts is totally and completely up to me.

I am not saying I was never down or depressed. When I left the hospital, there was almost nothing I could do for myself. I couldn't use the bathroom without help. And there were times I was frustrated and furious. I had never had great control over my temper, but in the first weeks after I left the hospital, I flew into a rage at the slightest thing.

One day, I wanted to leave the house, but I couldn't figure out a way to turn the doorknob. I was home alone, crying and screaming in anger and frustration. But even then, in the middle of such anger, I chose to take responsibility for myself. I kicked off my shoes and used my feet to work and work the knob until I got that door open. And in that moment, I realized this kernel of truth: It's not what happen to you that matters—it's what you do about it.

But even with my sincere belief in that philosophy and all my dedication to recovery, I still had one enormous hurdle to overcome. That was my concern about my face. I've had many surgeries to improve my appearance since then, but at the time, my face looked pretty hideous—especially in a society that believed men should all look like Tom Selleck. People's reactions were very difficult for me to handle. So when I was out in the street, I never met anyone's eyes. I just avoided that contact.

Then one day, I walked by an elementary school while the students were out on the playground. When they saw me, they came over to the fence and started shouting.

"Monster! Monster! You're a monster!" they shouted. The teacher immediately came over, forcing them inside and lecturing in a voice loud enough for me to hear about how rude they were.

I couldn't blame those kids. I did look like some kind of monster at that point. But nevertheless, I felt a tremendous sense of sadness and loss. I had an overwhelming desire to connect with those kids and let them know that on the inside, I was just like everyone else.

And it was at that moment that I found the focus for the rest of my life. I decided I would spend all my effort sharing my message of hope, challenge, and responsibility with adults and children all over the world. And that is exactly what I have done.

Right after that experience, I started learning to fly again. I couldn't really feed myself yet, and there were those people who thought I should learn to feed myself before I tried to fly. But I didn't want to just live; I wanted to experience life again. And that meant I had to fly. So I started learning how to work the controls with the finger stubs I had left. Before long, I was once again flying solo.

It was on vacation in Hawaii that I realized there was really nothing that I could not do. I decided I wanted to swim in the ocean. I knew that decision didn't make the greatest sense from some points of view. But that's what I wanted to do. So, convinced I was not going to drown, I jumped in the ocean and bodysurfed with the best of them. I was fine—better than fine. And that's when I decided that my accident was fully and completely behind me.

Not too long after that, I moved to Crested Butte, Colorado, a tiny town surrounded by tremendous physical beauty. I was ready to leave the big city and get connected to nature. And Crested Butte seemed the perfect place. The town was friendly and the scenery unsurpassed. And it was in Crested Butte that I heard from a friend about a business opportunity with a woodstove company in Vermont. I took a risk and decided to invest. I became a millionaire.

With my newfound fortune, I pursued my passion for flying. On November 11, 1975, I decided to fly my Cessna 206 to San Francisco to visit friends. It was the beginning of winter, and the plane, which had been stored outside, was icy. I thought my passengers and I had cleaned all the ice off the wings before we got in that morning. But we hadn't.

The plane crashed on take-off. And in that crash, I became paralyzed from the waist down. When the doctor told me I would be in a wheelchair for the rest of my life, I was devastated. I had fought for four long years to overcome my motorcycle accident. And now, this? It was too much.

But a friend from Crested Butte called me in the hospital and reminded me of some advice I had given her the previous year. It was advice she said helped her turn her life around, and she asked me if I still believed it.

"It's not what happens to you. It's what you do about it," she reminded me. And she was right. I decided then that if I could remake my life after my first accident, I could do it again. And so, I decided to just get on with it.

As best I could, I continued with my normal life in that rehab hospital. I made phone calls to my business interests all around the country. I had ice and drinks brought up for "happy hour." I organized trips to the local Mexican restaurant, and I flirted with as many nurses as possible. And soon, other patients caught on to the idea of actively choosing life.

But there was one young man who just never smiled. One day, I looked at him at said, "You know, before I was paralyzed, there were 10,000 things I could do. Now there are 9,000. What should I focus on? The 1,000 things I can't do? I prefer to focus on the 9,000 ways life can still be enjoyable and wonderful to me."

Since that time, I can hardly name all the things I have done and accomplished in my life. I got married, became mayor of Crested Butte, and ran for Congress. I've been flying and white-water rafting. I've done speaking engagements, radio, and TV all across the country.

But the most important thing I have accomplished in my life is motivational speaking—helping children and adults around the world see their potential, to encouraging them to act on their abilities. This is the work I truly love, and the work that consistently brings meaning to my own life. Sharing this always brings me joy and fulfillment.

The message about "the 9,000 things" is my legacy. It is this perspective I treasure more than anything else I have gathered in my life. Because this message teaches us that a tragedy in a life does not have to mean a life of tragedy.

"It's not what happens to you. It's what you do about it." Find out more about one of the top keynote speakers in the world by contacting: W Mitchell, 12014 West 54th Drive, Suite 100, Arvada, Colorado 80002. Tel: 303-425-1800. Fax: 303-425-9069. E-mail: mitchell@wmitchell.com. Web site: **www.wmitchell.com.**

One of W Mitchell's "9,000 things" is his involvement with the Emily Griffith Center, a special school for ten- to eighteen-year-old boys with emotional disturbances. Help these boys become self-reliant, open to learning, and experience meaningful hands-on practical growth opportunities. Contact: Emily Griffith Center, 14142 Denver West Parkway, #255, Golden, Colorado 80401. Tel: 303-277-1010. Fax: 303-277-1173. Web site: **www.unitedwaydenver.org/iris/tj0i9zrk.htm.**

In Canada, help to rebuild shattered lives by contacting The Canadian Paraplegic Association, 1101 Promenade Prince of Wales Drive, Suite 230, Ottawa, Ontario, K2C 3W7. Tel: 800-720-4933.

CHAPTER 16

Mike McLean 1996

Different Paths for Different Folks

LYNN WEISS

THROUGHOUT MY CHILDHOOD, all I knew was emotional pain. From the moment I had any consciousness, I felt anxiety and terror. I believed something was wrong at the very core of my being. I couldn't fit in. I didn't understand other kids. They didn't understand me. My parents didn't understand me. I didn't understand myself.

What I know now is that I was born with Attention Deficit Disorder (ADD). I was in pain for so many years simply because my brain wiring—and my needs, wants, talents, and joys—didn't fit into the very narrow mold that is considered acceptable in this culture. It took me decades of mental and spiritual exploration to understand that there is absolutely nothing wrong with me. And I am thankful that I've had the chance to help other people learn this lesson about themselves, too. ————————————————————

My parents weren't bad people; they just weren't very good at nurturing young life. I was their only child, and their expectations of me were formed even before I was born. I never really had a chance to live up to them.

My father wanted me to be successful at everything I did. So I worked as hard as I could to earn his love and attention. But it took every ounce of my energy to try to succeed in the way he would recognize. I struggled and struggled in school, terrified that I would fail.

On the outside, I looked successful. But the price I paid was a life of physical and emotional anxiety. I had no emotional energy left over to enjoy what we typically consider to be the innocence of childhood—running, jumping, exploring, dreaming. I used all my energy trying to be exactly who he wanted me to be. And when I didn't measure up, my father was an expert at piling on guilt.

My mother saw that I was different than the other children—that I thought about different things, that I didn't fit in socially. And she took that difference as a reflection of personal failure on her part. She wanted her child to be just like other children. She wanted her home to be just like the other homes, with glass figurines lined up just so on the coffee table. No fingerprints, nothing broken. But I wanted to touch the beautiful shapes and colors and feel their cool, smooth surfaces in my hands.

When I stepped out of the tight little box my mother drew around me, shame was her weapon of choice. "You're weird," she would say to me if I shared an idea that was different than what she expected. Or if I preferred to be by myself instead of playing with other children, she would ask, "What's the matter with you?"

As an adult, I once watched a home movie of myself from eighteen months to about four years old. I sobbed and sobbed as I watched, my heart just breaking for the precious child in that film. At eighteen months, I was bouncy, inquisitive, and happy. But by age three, I was stilted, awkward, always looking around to see if I was doing the right thing.

Occasionally, I did have an experience that allowed me to be fully myself. Our landlady, a former kindergarten teacher, often invited me down to her apartment before I started first grade. She had a wonderful box of crayons for me to use, and all kinds of small objects for me to draw around to make designs. Time stood still for me when I was at that table—lost in a world of shapes and colors and endless creative possibilities. Those were times of true and deep happiness. But they were rare.

I lived in a constant struggle to be someone I was not. I was a kinesthetic, experiential, hands-on learner trying to make my way in a linear, learn-it-from-a-textbook world. There was nothing wrong with the educational system I struggled in for so long—for some people. But there was everything wrong with it for me.

Consequently, every single day was a struggle as I fought to force someone else's teaching style into a brain that was wired to learn in a completely different way. But I kept on fighting. Always filled with anxiety and the fear of failure, I struggled all the way through college and graduate school, until I earned a doctorate. That's how badly I wanted to succeed in the eyes of the world.

That struggle left me very depressed. I went to a psychiatrist while I was in graduate school to try to find out why I felt so miserable, and she labeled me manic-depressive. Another doctor diagnosed me as paranoid schizophrenic. I was terrified.

Fortunately, I went for one more opinion. I found a psychiatrist who was able to help me. I told him about the diagnoses of the other doctors. And what he said to me that day brought me into a new life.

He took me by the shoulders and said, "Lynn, I don't want to ever hear you say that again. You are a healthy person. You do not have a mental illness—in any form."

That man, by this actions and words that day, and the counseling he provided me over a period of time, gave me a new life. He opened me up to the possibility that I was perfectly fine just the way I was. It was a possibility I had never considered.

This doctor helped me see the potential of life itself. And that's when I decided I wanted to work to help other people. I immediately felt absolutely passionate about that goal—it was even more important to me than trying to understand my own problems. So I began to study community mental health.

Community mental health was perfect for me. I was in a clinical setting working with people—it was hands-on, not theoretical. For the first time ever, school was easy. The fear, anxiety, and terror just went away. I instantly, instinctively knew what to do for my patients. I didn't even have to think about it. And the reason I was so successful is that I was learning in a setting that *fit* me. Finally. *This* was kinesthetic learning, learning by doing. I just soaked it all up.

Most important to me, though, I was *helping* people. Not helping because I tried to identify which textbook definition fit this or that person. But helping because my instincts—a gift of ADD—told me exactly what each person needed.

What I understand now is that what is labeled ADD is a perfectly natural way of being constructed. It has value equal to the linear way—it's just different. People who are wired linearly see and interpret life based on their very concrete five senses. People with ADD generally have a highly developed sensitivity. We are spontaneous, intuitive, and tend to be free spirits. Our emotions tend to be broad and expansive, rather than narrow and limited. And we tend to be creative thinkers and problem-solvers. Some people are a combination, with both ADD and linear brain wiring.

Once I started feeling my enormous possibilities, helping people became my passion. I knew I had something special to offer.

I remember one young woman I worked with, a teenager really. She had ADD attributes. She was suffering from severe depression. She told me someone had snubbed her at school. We talked about her feelings. It wasn't important whether or not this person had actually snubbed her. What was important was how it made her feel. I understood her sensitivity because of my own ADD.

We went for a walk in a nearby wooded area. We talked about how we would paint the leaves—how we would blend the paint. What I gave her was someone who would go off on flights of fancy with her. I reflected her inherent value. And she was able to see that.

"What are you passionate about?" I asked her. "What do you love?" And by working together, she began to trust that life could, indeed be a beautiful place.

I remember another young woman who had a phobia about school. I got in the car with her and drove her to school. On the first day, we got to school, I opened her car door, shut it, and we drove back home. The next day we walked halfway up the sidewalk—together. The next day, we walked into the classroom, again together. Her life changed in that glorious moment. Understanding her sensitivity and honoring it freed her to move forward.

She did have some serious family issues, too. So I helped her find ways of interacting with her family that worked for her. Being sensitive, she perceived her dad as being gruff and hardened. I showed her how to keep her sensitivity, but be able to interact with her family members without getting hurt. When her father would say something in a gruff tone to her, she learned to ask, "Dad, what do you mean?" She discovered that her father had a kind heart. And once she realized that, they connected for the first time.

These days, I am working with some prison inmates in a minimum-security facility, some of whom have been identified as having ADD attributes. I love working with these people. When I look at them, I am so clear that "there but for the grace of God go I." Generally speaking, these are simply people who have not been blessed with the kind of opportunities that they needed in order to learn and function well. These are people who do not know who they are. And while they are trying to figure that out, I am the lucky one who can share part of that journey with them.

As I am teaching them, they are wonderful teachers for me, too. The very first day, I came in with an organized lesson plan. And after just a few minutes, I realized I needed to throw all that out. I needed to just use my intuition to go with the flow. Once again, I have been shown that I need to trust, and benefit from, my unique thinking style.

In my ADD coaching, I noticed one man in particular whom the staff had labeled as oppositional. Every time he would be told to do something in class, he would ask, "Why?" The staff saw that as a bad attitude, but I saw it as something else.

I went over and sat down with this man. Before long, I realized he was asking, "Why?" because he needed to see the big picture in order to understand why he was being asked to do a particular exercise in class. He wasn't satisfied just seeing a narrow slice of the picture; he needed to see the big picture for the assignment to make sense to him. Since recognizing that, I've been able to help the staff understand where his questions are coming from. And I've helped this man understand how to phrase those questions in a different tone and manner. Now everyone's needs are being met.

These inmates and so many other people I've been fortunate to work with continually remind me how easy it is for all of us with ADD attributes to misunderstand and to be misunderstood. An important ADD attribute is our highly developed sixth sense, our intuition. I encourage people to use their intuitive nature to guide them on the right path, the one that fits. I encourage them to learn to trust their feelings and honor them.

These are the lessons I share with others through my work—and the lessons others are continually teaching me as well. Life is a continual journey, and by using my unique abilities, the very ones I always considered liabilities, it is a journey filled with adventure and joy. And for that I am constantly thankful.

Find out what you can do to help a child or adult with different learning styles by contacting: Educare, 201 Ridgewood, San Marcos, Texas 78666. Tel: 512-393-3288. E-mail: educaretraining@yahoo.com. In Canada, contact the Newell Community Action Group, Box 63, 327 3rd Street West, Brooks, AB TIR IB2. Tel: 403-362-6661.

CHAPTER 17

Susan Kandell 1999

On the Way Home

BEN BELTZER

I N 1974, I DID SOMETHING I HAD BEEN TAUGHT never to do. I made a business deal and sealed it with a handshake. Now, I knew better than that. My father had always taught me to be careful, to use attorneys, to use accountants, to sign contracts, to get everything in writing. But for some reason, I sealed that deal with a handshake.

It was a mistake that cost me almost everything. A mistake that led me to despair, depression, and very nearly to suicide. But it was also a mistake that eventually led me into a new life—a life more wonderful than I had ever been able to imagine.

So was that handshake really a mistake? I think only God knows the answer to that one. _____

It all started because I knew a man who had a failing business, and I thought I could turn it around. So we made a deal. I would take over his business and make it a success. If I did, he would compensate me with 85 percent of the company's stock.

I certainly kept my part of the bargain. I worked day and night for several years, and the business became very successful. I also found a buyer for it and sold the business for him. But when I asked for my 85 percent compensation, the previous owner said we had never agreed to anything in writing. He took all the money from the sale and left me with only four parting words: "Thank you very much."

Up until that moment, I had always been successful in business—and in life in general. I was forty years old, living an affluent lifestyle with my wife and four children in Liberty, Missouri. We had a five-bedroom home and nice cars. We had always been active and generous in our church. We were well respected in the community.

But suddenly, I was the one in need. I couldn't even find a job. I went on interview after interview, but no one could pay me the salary I needed to support four children. After a year with no income, we lost everything—our home, our cars, everything. With four children in high school, we moved into a one-bedroom apartment.

It was while I was in line at the welfare office and the unemployment office that I first really became familiar with poor people. I had always thought that poor people were somehow "different" than the rest of us, but suddenly I began to realize we were all the same. I had hunger pangs. They had hunger pangs. I was in pain because I wasn't able to care for my family. And they were in pain. What I discovered was that poor people were loving and caring people. They were genuine and honest. And now I was one of them.

Nothing in my previous life had prepared me to live on welfare, at the mercy of the state. And nothing had prepared me to deal with the feelings of worthlessness and despair that I carried around with me twenty-four hours a day. I became convinced that my family really would be better off without me.

One day, I drove out to a retreat center. I parked my car and walked around the back of the building, behind the chapel. I sat down, pulled a gun out of my coat, and I pointed it at my head. I was absolutely ready to pull that trigger.

But just then, I felt a hand on my shoulder. It was a friend of mine named Matthew. He had called my wife to check on me, and she told him I had left the house very depressed. He found me just in time.

I'm not sure how glad I was to see Matthew at that moment. I wanted to escape from the unbearable pain I was feeling—from the burden I had become to my family—and he kept me from that. But now I am so thankful. And I know now that God sent Matthew that day because He had work for me to do.

It was soon after that experience that I finally got my first job—at a gas station. With a college degree, I was pumping gas outside in the winter at minimum wage, working for a manager who was twenty-five years my junior. I was glad to have the job—but I was still angry, disillusioned, and depressed.

Not too long afterward, though, I heard about an opportunity to buy a service station. I had only debts at that point, so I knew I couldn't afford it. But I prayed about it, and then let it go. Then amazingly, a member of my church came forward and loaned me the money. I had never thought I would have an opportunity to own my own business again. I was so thankful.

As I was getting my new business going, I thought long and hard about my recent experiences. I began to see that God had been trying to send me a message. I knew the message had something to do with working with the poor, but I didn't know exactly what to do. So at a worship service one Sunday, I asked if anyone in the congregation wanted to meet with me to talk about the issues of the poor.

Four people showed up at that first meeting, and that included my wife. But I wasn't discouraged. We might have been a small group, but we were serious about our goal. The five of us established a mission group.

Since we didn't know yet exactly what direction to take, we decided to focus our attention first on our inward journey, the journey of the soul. We began to read Scripture daily, keep journals, and spend two hours a week working with the impoverished. We did that for nine months, meeting weekly to discuss what we were learning. It was a time of tremendous spiritual growth. And we began to realize that God was calling us to work with homeless people.

We decided that our goal would be to help homeless folks learn to meet their own needs. I knew that self-esteem can only thrive when you can take care of yourself and your own family. And so that's how Hillcrest Ministries was born.

As our plans began to take shape, we decided we needed an apartment building where the homeless could stay while taking advantage of the skills we would teach. In 1975, one of our congregants helped us buy our first apartment building. We knew this was what God wanted us to do—and the program we started then is still going strong today.

About ten years later, the mayor of Dallas challenged the city to solve its problem of housing for the homeless. Two churches stepped forward to answer that call. And, as fate would have it, my daughter was on the board of one of those churches. She told them about Hillcrest Ministries, and they asked me to come to Dallas and set up a program. I prayed about it and felt the calling to respond to those needs. In 1985, we moved to Dallas, and the Interfaith Housing Coalition was founded to provide transitional housing and services for homeless people.

These days, I work sixty to seventy hours per week for less money than I have ever earned in my life—with the exception of the time I worked at that gas station. And my life looks a bit crazy from the outside. One minute I'm wearing a suit and tie, and the next minute I'm in my jeans scrubbing an apartment to get it ready for a new family. My title at Interfaith is executive director, which sounds pretty fancy. But I do everything from talking to the media to cleaning bathrooms.

When people first come to the Interfaith Housing Coalition, they generally feel unlovable. Their appearance is horrible and their language is nasty. But we give them love. We give them shelter and food. And we help them learn to take care of themselves. We help them study for their GED test. We teach them about budgets and personal finance. We help them learn the skills they need to hold a job, and we talk about how to interview for a job.

We also have after-school tutoring for the children. And we talk about parenting and child care—because many of our children come from situations that are so abusive, it's hard to believe.

But the most important thing we do for our residents is that we love them. No matter what else we do, love is the key. And, in turn, I know that being with them and watching the positive changes in their lives gives me the greatest happiness and peace.

The truth is that I've never been happier in my life. I realized that after spending time one day with one of our youngest residents, a little boy named Christopher.

Every morning I arrive early at the Interfaith apartments to have some quiet time, quiet time I use for prayer. This one particular morning, though, I heard a child who just wouldn't stop crying.

So I said to God, "God, this is our time. Will you please quiet this child so you and I can have our time?" But instead of the child getting quieter, he got louder. So I went to check it out.

I found Christopher standing at the front door to his apartment, with one overall strap on and one off. His mother was across the street with his little brother, waiting for the bus to take his brother to the child care center. This was her first day of work and Christopher's first day to get on the school bus all by himself.

I fixed Christopher's clothes, took him to my apartment, made him breakfast, and took him to school. When Christopher came back to the apartment building in the afternoon—the Interfaith van picks up the children after school—he found me. And he followed me around like I was the Pied Piper. I was cleaning an apartment, getting it ready for a new family, putting fresh flowers on the kitchen table, and Christopher wanted to help. I told him that this is what we did for his apartment before his family came to Interfaith Housing. I told him that we always clean the apartment, and we always pray for a new family before they come.

After we finished cleaning, I opened the door to leave. But Christopher grabbed my hand and said, "We haven't prayed." And he took me to the bedroom and knelt by the bed. I knelt down beside him and we prayed together for a family we had not even met yet.

About three days later, as I was driving down the street, I suddenly had a tremendous revelation: Christopher didn't need me—I needed him!

We think we have so much to give the poor. But it's really they who have so much to give us.

Some days, I think back to that fateful handshake—the one that almost cost me my life. What would have happened if I had used a legal document to seal that business arrangement instead of a handshake? You know, they say the Lord works in mysterious ways. But I usually put it in simpler terms.

God is pretty neat. And I am so thankful.

Break the cycle of homelessness and help people get their lives back on track. Contact: Interfaith Housing Coalition, P. O. Box 720206, Dallas, Texas 75372-0206. Tel: 214-827-7220. Fax: 214-827-1347. In Canada, contact the United Way, serving 200 social service agencies that help the homeless, abused women and children, senior citizens in need, and others. Located at 26 Wellington Street East, Toronto, Ontario, M5E 1W9.

Rocky Powell 1998

Angel on My Shoulder

NANCY BRINKER

I HAD THE MOST AMAZING SISTER. They just don't come any better than Susan Goodman Komen. She was kind, gentle, and beautiful. She was patient and loving and fair. She was the older sister who never seemed to mind having her younger sister tag along. We were loving and close as children, and even closer as adults.

When Suzy and I were little, we used to dream about what our lives would be like when we grew up. We imagined handsome husbands, wonderful children, nice homes. What we didn't dream about was breast cancer and the overwhelming role it would play in our adult lives. But neither did we dream that together, we would have the opportunity to do so much good for so many people. ⸻

Suzy and I had an incredibly simple yet happy childhood in Peoria, Illinois, in the 1950s. We lived in a *Father Knows Best* world on a quiet, tree-lined street, where everyone knew everyone else. Our father was clearly the head of the household. Our mother was a good-humored Girl Scout leader, PTA member, and volunteer in every charitable organization you could think of. And, as hard as this is to believe these days, she was usually in the kitchen baking cookies when Suzy and I came home from school. She taught us by example to share, to always help those who didn't have enough, and that if you were given a good life, it was an obligation to lead by example

Suzy was the perfect child. Really. She was kind and helpful and considerate and cute and cuddly. She was the high-school homecoming queen, the college beauty queen. And through all that well-deserved adulation, Suzy was just as nice as she could be. She was always, and sincerely, concerned about helping other people. She was the one who remembered everyone's birthday. She was the one who was always doing the sweet little things for people that the rest of us glossed over.

I, on the other hand, was the big, gangly one who never seemed quite to fit in. While Suzy did some modeling, I was the "bookish" tomboy who much preferred reading or galloping around on a horse all day long. The truth is that I was in college before I really felt confident and comfortable with myself.

After college, Suzy came back to Peoria. She married Stan Komen, her college sweetheart. But I had no desire to stay in such a small town. I decided to move to Dallas. I had visited an aunt there as a child and I loved the idea of living in Texas' wide open spaces.

As I was interested in learning marketing and business, I immediately got a job at Neiman Marcus, which is where I met my first husband. Although the marriage was not good, and we later divorced, it was through that marriage that I was blessed with my son, Eric.

Suzy and I talked to each other every day in the late afternoon during those years. Although we were physically far apart, we loved each other more than ever. We shared everything about our lives. We discussed our husbands, our children, our careers, the news in Peoria and Dallas. And most importantly, we laughed a lot. Hearing her voice at the other end of the phone was a treasure to me. I knew I could turn to her to share my joys. I could turn to her to share my problems.

But then there was the phone call on a Tuesday afternoon in 1977. The call I will never forget. Suzy's doctor had discovered a lump in her breast—a lump that was not a cyst. He wanted to do a biopsy right away. Suzy told me it was no big deal, but I decided to fly to Peoria to be with her. By the time I got off the plane, my father's face gave me the news no one ever wants to hear: My sister had cancer.

Suzy had lived in a relatively small town almost all her life and had been cared for by the same doctor the entire time. This man knew her and knew the family. He was wonderful and friendly, and Suzy trusted him completely. So she immediately trusted the surgeon he called in to review her case.

The surgeon told Suzy he could cure her of cancer by removing some of the interior breast tissue, replacing it with an implant and leaving the outer tissue and skin intact. All she wanted was to know that she could put this cancer behind her and go back to being a healthy wife and mother. He told her exactly what she wanted to hear. He used the word "cure."

The problem—the very, very serious problem—was that neither of these doctors were cancer specialists. I know they both wanted to take good care of Suzy. But they really were not capable of giving her the best treatment possible. I wanted Suzy to get another opinion, to go to a major comprehensive cancer center. But she wanted to stay in Peoria, and the decision was ultimately hers.

Within six months of her surgery, the cancer had spread to her lungs and under her arm. That's when she went to the Mayo Clinic in Rochester, Minnesota, and the M. D. Anderson Cancer Center in Houston. She was treated with radiation and told to have her ovaries removed. But nothing seemed to stop the cancer that was raging in her body.

Through it all, Suzy retained her sense of dignity, her sense of humor, and her deep concern for other people. When she was physically able to, she would sit and visit with other cancer patients who were too weak to leave their beds. She would listen to their problems. She was concerned about how other women felt sitting in the bleak, depressing waiting rooms. She was concerned about other women having to go through what she had been through.

"Nanny," she said to me one day—she used to call me Nanny—"breast cancer is wrong. You've got to fix this. You've got to do something to make sure no other family ever goes through what we went through. You've got to help me fix this."

"I will, Suzy," I said, with absolutely no idea how I could possibly accomplish what she was asking of me. "If it takes the rest of my life, I'll make sure it gets done."

That was one of the last conversations I ever had with my sister. After a three-year battle, Suzy died of breast cancer at age thirty-six. She left behind her parents, a loving husband, two wonderful children, and a sister who will never, ever stop missing her and loving her.

I was torn apart in every direction when Suzy died. My job had come to an end, I was going through the end of a painful divorce with a man who was fighting me for custody of my child, and Suzy's death left me with a deeper sadness and loneliness than I could ever have imagined.

But in addition to my grief, I was absolutely outraged. I was outraged by the lack of information about breast cancer, by the lack of treatment options, and by the lack of empowerment Suzy had as a patient.

And I realized then that I had a choice to make. I could focus on my rage or bring attention to these issues of breast cancer and the lack of concern about this disease. I could try to fix what was wrong.

The choice was clear to me. I had made a promise to my sister. And, anyway, Suzy and I had been raised to be fixers.

From the time we were little, riding around with Mother in an old beat-up station wagon, she told us, "This is your country. If you think something is wrong with it, it's up to you girls to fix it. Don't complain. If you want something done, get off your duff and do it."

And from the time we were little, that's what we did. Suzy and I did our first fund-raiser when she was nine and I was six. Some of our neighborhood friends and children at school had been stricken with polio. That was the terrible disease of our generation, and Suzy and I wanted to do something about it. So we put together a little singing and dancing variety show with the neighborhood kids, and we called it the Polio Benefit Show.

Suzy and I raised $64 from our performances. And I will never forget the joy we felt inside when Mother took us to the Polio Association to give them that check.

So when I faced that choice during the months after Suzy's death—to focus on my rage or try to fix the problems—the answer was clear. Suzy had told me to fix it. And what's what I would do.

After I made my decision, I had absolutely no idea how to get started. So I just mulled it over for a while. Then my new husband, Norman, whom I married shortly after Suzy's death, reminded me that I had quite a bit of fund-raising experience, skills I could put to good use here. And he was right.

In 1982, with the help of a few friends who also had personal ties to breast cancer, I established the Susan G. Komen Breast Cancer Foundation. We started with a few hundreds dollars and a shoebox full of friend's names. We got on the phone. And over time, we planned luncheons and gala fund-raisers and developed what turned into the Race for the Cure®.

What the Foundation really had going for it was my burning desire to right the wrongs I had experienced through Suzy's battle. I knew we had to raise money for breast cancer research and education. We needed to empower women to make truly informed choices. And we needed to fix up those waiting rooms so the frightened women sitting there would never have to feel degraded as an additional burden. Along the way, I developed breast cancer myself. Fortunately, I had learned a lot, and had earlier treatment.

Our army of volunteers has grown from that original handful to thousands of people working through our affiliate network in more than 104 cities. Now, more than 700,000 people across the country run in the Race for the Cure® each year. And we have been able to fund millions of dollars worth of research grants. In fact, the Komen Foundation is now the nation's largest private funder of research dedicated solely to breast cancer.

Have I fulfilled my promise to my sister? We're not there yet. We're closer to the finish line, but we're not there yet.

In all the years I have worked with the Komen Foundation, I have felt that there's something bigger than me at work here. I feel like Suzy is an angel, always watching over our shoulders. I feel like she's there with me all the time. I can't explain it. But when I feel down, if something goes wrong, I just know that Suzy is right there with me. There are so many times I feel her presence. Suzy isn't in her physical form any more, but I know she's there.

I believe that each of us is guided by something positive—call it goodwill, call it angels, call it positive energy. It's something that keeps us fulfilled in the spiritual sense. Watching the Komen Foundation grow—watching all these things happen that were beyond even my wildest expectations—the experience has been so full of goodwill and love that it's truly amazing.

Nobody's life is meant to be easy. And sometimes adversity makes you a better person. I still feel badly that Suzy didn't have more time on this earth, particularly time to spend with her children. But the gift she gave me in death—the challenge she held up to me—is the gift she has given to the world.

If Suzy could talk to me now, I know just what she would say. "Oh my God—we've done an incredible job, Nanny," she would say. "We have to keep going until we 'fix breast cancer.'"

Let's fight breast cancer the best way we know how...TOGETHER. For more information, contact: The Susan G. Komen Breast Cancer Foundation, 5005 LBJ Freeway, Suite 370, Dallas, Texas 75244. Tel: 972-855-1600. Fax: 972-855-1605. Web site: **www.komen.org.** In Canada, contact Willow, a resource and support center for women with breast cancer and their families. Located at 590 Jarvis Street, 5th Floor, Toronto, Ontario, M4Y 2J4. Tel: 416-962-8881. Fax: 416-962-8084. E-mail: comcoord@ywcacanada.ca

Susan Kandell 1999

His Brother's Keeper

JEFF MOYER

I GUESS A LOT OF PEOPLE CAN'T REMEMBER being five years old—but I can. In fact, I can never forget it. I lived in Cleveland with my parents and sister. And two things happened during that summer that changed my life forever.

I think most people would see those two events as painful and damaging. And I agree they have been painful. But damaging? No. It is only by working through them that I was able to become the person I was always meant to be. _____

The summer I was five years old I got the measles. And a baby brother.

I remember becoming very sick in July of that year and having a high fever that the doctor couldn't seem to bring down. I was sick for a long time. When I was finally well enough to go outside, I remember playing soap bubbles with my sister near our house. I was frustrated with the bubbles because they were breaking apart so quickly. One minute they would be there, and then when I looked again, they would be gone.

"What are you talking about?" my sister asked when I complained to her. "The air is still full of bubbles."

That was the first time I was aware that what I was seeing was different from other people. It didn't bother me in particular. It's just the way things were.

When my parents noticed I was having trouble seeing, they took me to an optometrist. I will never forget that examination.

"There's nothing wrong with Jeff," the man told my parents, after looking in my eyes. "He's just pretending that he can't see."

And since that's what the doctor said, that's what my parents believed.

In August of that same summer, my brother Mark was born. I remember my father coming back from the hospital without any of the joy on his face I expected. He didn't seem happy at all—just worried. When they brought Mark home from the hospital, a sense of depression settled over our home. My mother seemed shaken. She told me Mark had retardation. I didn't know what that meant, but I did know that it was making my parents very sad.

As we watched Mark develop over the next few years, we were all aware of the delays he experienced because of his retardation. I knew my parents were upset. But I wasn't. I thought Mark was fine just the way he was.

My own life became more and more complicated as my vision loss progressed. Since no one believed I had a physical problem, I felt obligated even as a young child to pretend that nothing was wrong. I would play baseball to try to be like the other kids—and deal with the tremendous anxiety that came from not being able to see the ball. I took piano lessons, even though I couldn't see the music. And I tried to do my best in school, even though I couldn't see what was written on the board.

Mark's problems, too, increased as he got older. He wanted to interact with other children, but the neighborhood kids were cruel to him.

I especially remember the first time I baby-sat Mark by myself. He was about two years old, and we went out in the yard to play. A neighbor boy who was my age came over and looked at Mark.

"What's the matter with him?" he asked. I told him nothing was the matter with him. And this boy reached over and shoved Mark down to the ground.

I jumped on that kid, and I jumped on him hard. It was the only time in my life I have ever used violence. I let him know that he was never going to treat my brother like that again. He made me realize—for the first of many, many times—that my brother was so very vulnerable. No one in that neighborhood ever tried to hurt Mark again.

By this time, I had lost about 90 percent of my vision, and my family and teachers finally began to take my problem seriously. I was hospitalized for a week, but they still couldn't come up with a diagnosis. I was glad that my parents believed me, finally, but we were never able to really talk about it. Maybe they just didn't want to believe it.

So I kept trying to do all the normal things I thought I should be doing—play sports, join Scouting—but it was a very, very painful and lonely time for me. I believed that if I just tried hard enough, I could see. So I tried and tried. I even kept practicing baseball, throwing the ball up and trying to catch it. But I just couldn't see. One time, when the ball came down, it broke my nose. I was so frustrated and so ashamed, I didn't even tell my parents what happened.

But worse than my own problems were my worries about Mark. We had moved to a new area of town, and the children in that neighborhood just tortured him. They hit him with croquet mallets, even while one of their parents was looking. When they played house, they forced my brother to be the dog and would tie him to the tree by his neck. One day, when they told him to run into the street to chase a ball, he was hit by a car and broke his leg.

I was struck by the terrible inequity of the situation. How could I protect my brother if I were losing my sight? How could God allow me to go blind and let my brother suffer so much? So I made a bargain with God. I told Him that I would agree to go blind if He would just restore my brother's mind. We were a pretty strong Methodist family, but Mark's circumstances made me question the justice of the universe.

In 1962, my parents realized there was no place in the public school system for a child like Mark. And he had been rejected from every private school they had applied to. They looked for other options, but there were none at that time. And so, based on the advice my parents were given, when he was eight, Mark was institutionalized outside of Cleveland.

Mark's living situation horrified me. More than 4,500 people lived in the buildings, which dated to the time of the Civil War. The room he slept in had fifty beds in it. And the room he sat in during the day had fifty chairs. He had no privacy of any kind. He was beaten many times and even thrown down the fire escape. When we would come to visit, Mark would arrive dressed in dirty rags.

By the time I was sixteen, my vision had deteriorated to the point that I was no longer allowed to ride a bike, play football, wrestle, or dive into a pool for fear that any blow to my head would cause me to lose whatever sight remained. Everything a sixteen-year-old boy wanted to do was taken away from me. But whenever I felt sorry for myself, I thought of Mark.

One of the very few things in my life that brought me solace was music. I realized I could play guitar by ear. I had been writing poetry for years, and at sixteen, I started writing songs. I wrote about my brother's institutionalization and other disability issues. I wrote about civil rights and peace, and I started playing the coffee house circuit.

I left home at age nineteen with $400, my guitar, and a backpack. I left behind my parents and two quarters of college. And although I didn't want to, I left Mark behind, too. I wasn't really sure I could make it on my own, but I left anyway. And I went to California.

I had never been able to compete academically, but I found out that at the

University of California at Berkeley, there was a special section in the library where I could study with tapes and readers. I could also get more time on tests and other accommodations for my vision loss. The fertile world of academia finally opened up to me. I worked hard. I made all As and graduated with a degree in social welfare.

And I became very involved in the disability rights movement. I was hired by the Center for Independent Living in Berkeley and began to become seriously involved in the political effort to expand civil rights for people with disabilities.

I was still writing songs, and began to write more about disability issues. I also started volunteering to teach guitar to kids with blindness or low vision. And I saw that through music, I could really make a contribution. I could use my music to change people's thoughts and feelings, to change their lives.

But all through this time—even while my life was finally coming together—I continued to worry about Mark. The suffering I knew he lived with was like an open wound to me, but I could only get home to see him about once a year. So in 1982, after studying and working in California for almost ten years, I moved back to Cleveland to see what I could do for Mark.

By that time, my father had died, and my mother's second husband helped me get Mark out of the institution he had been in for so long. We moved him to a different institution in Cleveland, an hour away from where I lived. Eventually, I was able to get him into a group home. The situation was still not great, but it was better.

Two years later, in 1992, my eye disease was finally correctly diagnosed. I was told I had a progressive retinal degeneration that would lead to blindness.

A lot of things in my life came to an end that year. I was rapidly losing more vision. Nothing could be done to stop the process. I felt I had to leave my job and my career, due to an ethical impasse with my boss. And my personal relationships also suffered and fell apart. In a way, everything in my life came to a grinding halt. But even as I was feeling this tremendous sense of loss and grieving over so many issues, I also realized exactly what I had to do with my life.

All through the years, I had been using my vacation time to perform my music addressing disability rights and the wholeness of all people. Suddenly I realized I needed to be speaking and performing about those issues full-time. I was teetering on bankruptcy, mortgaged to the hilt, and had no real work coming in, but I believed deep in my heart that educating people about disability rights was exactly what I was supposed to be doing.

And so I started performing, traveling, and teaching wherever I could. Now, just by word of mouth, I work all over the country. I've published workbooks and recordings. I perform for students of all ages. I share poems and music and stories. I feel blessed to be able to do this. My music, my blindness, and my devotion to civil rights all came together to bring me to this point.

But it is my brother who has been my greatest teacher. I have seen his soul burnished, polished, and deepened by the pain he has been through. Yes, he displays a rage from time to time that can only come from the years of torture he has lived through. And Mark's rage is a constant reminder for me to keep working for a day when no child has to live as he did. But Mark can also be the most generous, loving, forgiving, and gentle human being I know.

My blindness has been my other great teacher. It has forced me to let go of the illusions of the outer world, and focus on my inner life. I can't see what people look like, so I don't judge by appearance. And that is a liberating gift. Blindness has brought me into true contact with others, by allowing myself to be physically guided by them. And by giving others the opportunity to help me, I am giving them an opportunity to be of service. That viewpoint has taken a lot of time to develop. I no longer feel dependent on others—it is the dance of interdependence.

So my blindness is not about loss. It's about working on behalf of everyone who is seen as different, deviant, ridiculed, or excluded. It's about living my life in a way that reflects the dignity of everyone.

The sad truth is that my mother never realized that my brother and I are whole, and always have been. Blindness and retardation do not define us. Yes, those are aspects of who we are. But they are only attributes—not the entire picture. My life's work is to help people recognize the wholeness of all people, regardless of their capabilities.

When my mother died, I became Mark's legal guardian. And I was finally able to get him into a living situation where he had his own room. For the first time in his life, he had a place for his own things where they wouldn't be stolen—a place he could call home.

But 100,000 Americans still live in state institutions. We wouldn't accept the conditions they live in for ourselves or our own children. But, as a society, we think it's OK for people with retardation to live in these places because we devalue people with disabilities. And when we devalue people, we stop seeing them.

The goal of my life now, the meaning of my life, is to teach people to truly see each other. We are each whole people, regardless of our particular abilities. Our value is intrinsic, within us as the birthright of being human. I hope that my work can lift understanding and help others start seeing from the inside out.

Help Jeff spread his message of wholeness. For more information, contact: Music from the Heart, 670 Radford Drive, Cleveland, Ohio 44163-1905. Tel: 440-442-2779. Fax: 440-449-4652. E-mail: moyer@jeffmoyer.com Web site: **www.jeffmoyer.com.**

J. Kevin Wolfe 1998

The Spirit War Can't Destroy

NADJA HALILBEGOVICH

U NTIL I WAS TWELVE YEARS OLD, I lived a life of luxury in Sarajevo, the beautiful city of the Winter Olympics and the capital of Bosnia-Herzegovina. Our city was filled with trees and flowers and kind people everywhere. We had music and art. And to complete the picture, everywhere we looked we saw the majesty of the mountains all around the city. Sarajevo was perfect to me in every way.

But everything changed one morning in 1992. That was the day that prejudice and intolerance exploded into bullets and grenades. And for four years, our lives were torn apart by war. For all those who died—for all the children who never lived to see the age I am now, nineteen—I am committed to helping others learn the lessons that will prevent this from happening again. _____

Before the war, in the easy years of my childhood, I lived with my parents and my older brother, Sanel, in a beautiful apartment on the fourteenth floor of a building in an upper-middle-class neighborhood. My mother was a business manager at the National Bank of Bosnia-Herzegovina, and my father was a manager at a major book company. In addition to our wonderful apartment, we had a house in a nearby village where we spent our sun-filled weekends, a small apartment, some land on the island of Brach in the Adriatic Sea, and two nice cars. Every winter, Sanel and I would go skiing for two weeks. And every summer, the whole family would vacation for a month.

I had every advantage a child could dream of. I was a good student at a good school filled with my friends. I took private guitar lessons. I sang in the choir. I loved every part of my life.

And then, on April 5, 1992, the shooting began. On that day, and the four years of nightmare that followed it, my Sarajevo and my childhood were savagely ripped from my grasp. That was the day when hatred poured into our city, when people who had been living together for years in peace could no longer get along. That was the day some fanatic Orthodox Serbs decided that Muslims like my family, as well as many Jews and Christians, no longer had a place in this land of our hearts.

I woke up that morning, just like every other day, and walked into the dining room before school. The minute I saw my parents' faces, I knew something was very wrong.

"Nadja, I'm sorry, but you won't be going to school today," they said. "Barricades are being set up in the city. The gates are being closed. It's not safe to go outside." Those were their words. But their faces said even more, much more.

Just a few months earlier, we had heard about fighting in neighboring Croatia. We were so shocked. While we waited for news of our friends, we collected gifts for the children there. Now, I can see the fighting in Croatia as a warning of what was coming our way. At the time, though, we never thought it could happen to us.

But soon, I became one of the children who would need a gift or package of food sent from a stranger far away.

In those first few weeks, I believed the craziness would end soon. I believed the men with their ski masks and guns would just go away. I believed the sound of gunfire, the terrifying trips to the safety of our cold basement, the blood I saw in the street with my own eyes—I believed all of it would end soon. But after months, and then years, filled with smoke and blood, I felt it would never end.

By the end of the war, my life had changed so much that I had to force myself to remember what it had been like before. What were those foods we ate? Foods so plentiful they covered the entire tabletop—what were they made of? What was it like to go outside and play with friends, to feel the sunshine on my face? What did my beautiful city look like before all the trees had been chopped down for firewood? And what did it sound like when the birds sat in those trees and sang for us? Where had all the birds gone?

For us, there was no flying away to another town, no flying up into the mountains to escape. No one was allowed to leave the city without signed papers. And we could not get papers.

As hard as it was for me to believe, we adjusted to living with war. Before long, we stopped running to the basement every time we heard gunfire. We learned when it might be safe to stay in the apartment, and when it was really necessary for us to hide in the dark basement with the horrible moldy walls. We learned to get along without sugar or fresh fruit. We learned to eat black beans one night and red the next, then black, then red, then black again, to pretend we were eating a variety of foods. And as children, we learned to ignore the pain in our toes when we stuffed our feet every day into shoes we had outgrown the previous year.

But one thing I never learned how to do was how to stop worrying about my mother. Even in the middle of the war, she woke up every day, put makeup on her beautiful face, got dressed, and went out the door to work. My father had been fired from his job at the beginning of the war because he was not a Serb. My mother had been allowed to keep her job, but she worked through the entire war without pay.

I tried not to cry as I saw her go each morning. But if fifteen people were murdered in the street that day, or thirty-five—or even one—how did I know it would not be my precious mother?

My mother said she went to work every day because she would die if she became a prisoner in her own home. And so I learned to let her go. And every day at 3 P.M., I sat by the apartment door, waiting to hear the sound of her footsteps. That was the sound that brought me joy and told me my own small family was still safe—at least for a few more hours.

Sometimes I slept on the floor by that door at night, because we believed it was one of the most secure places in our apartment. My mother would sit with me for a while in the dark, while we listened to the shells exploding all around us. Her warm hands and beautiful eyes were the only things that made me feel safe. And eventually, with the sounds of war all around me, I would drift off to sleep.

Before the war, I would have been so happy to have a day without school—just like any child. But when the war started, all I wanted was the normal life of going to school with my friends, seeing my beloved teachers, and learning so many wonderful things.

Some days, a teacher would volunteer her time to meet with us in the stairwells in the apartment buildings. On other days, we would all risk our lives—teachers and students—to meet together in a small room in a building not far from the school. And on the radio, sometimes there would be special quizzes where you could call in the answers. I loved those quizzes. My father and I sat at the dining room table with reference books piled high all around us. When we heard the questions on the radio, we would look so fast through the books to try to find the information we needed—and then see if we could be the first one to call in the answer.

I didn't want to fall behind the other children of Europe just because of the war. I studied Bosnian, English, French, geography, math, chemistry, and anything else I could get my hands on. I lived through the books I read and the things I learned. That's how I nourished my inner life.

Learning—and music. It was during the war that I began to learn the classics—Mozart, Schubert, and Bach. I loved the way music took me beyond my prison.

I also loved my diary like a friend, a friend I could pour out my heart and soul to. I wrote my first entry about seven weeks after the war started, and I wrote on and off for the next four years. When I was frightened by the news or by the snipers in the streets, I would pour my fears into my diary. When I was elated because my mother had been able to scrape together some ingredients to make a cake, I shared my joy with my diary.

Then I was wounded. That fateful day was Sunday, October 18, 1992. I had gone out to play in our courtyard, to feel the sunshine on my arms. Suddenly, there was a blast above my head, and thick black smoke was everywhere. At first, I couldn't see anything and I screamed and screamed in panic. Then I saw a large piece of wall dangling from our building.

I felt dizzy. I ran toward the building, screaming and crying. My legs were in pain, and when I touched them, I felt blood. I saw my neighbor and threw my arms around her neck. She dragged me to her doorstep while blood from my legs trailed behind us, and then she wrapped my legs. I heard people calling my name loudly, but I was fading in and out of consciousness. Then I heard the wonderful voice of my father.

At the hospital, we saw so many people who were worse off than I was. The boy sitting next to me was having shrapnel taken out of his back without anesthesia. Finally, the doctors saw me and told me I did not have to have my legs amputated. They bandaged my legs and my father found a friend to take us home.

I felt so bad about all the supplies they used on me because I knew there was such a shortage.

When we arrived at our building, my nineteen-year-old brother, Sanel, took me in his arms and cried like a child. We had no electricity for the elevator, so he carried me in his arms up fourteen flights of stairs. Now I realize what a burden I must have been to him. But at the time, all I thought about was how much we loved each other.

It was a long recovery, but with the help of so many people who loved me, I started walking again.

A year and a half later, we thought the war was over. With the help of the UN troops, we felt the possibility of peace coming back into our lives. We rejoiced in the springtime, we smiled in the sun. I believed that my childhood had returned. Instead, after a brief period of time, what returned was war.

In July 1995, God answered some of my prayers. In response to a letter my mother wrote to the Bosnian Humanitarian Organization in Croatia, we heard that an American family was willing to host me in their home so I could continue my education. I was endlessly happy. Even knowing that it meant tearing myself from my beloved family, I knew I had to go.

But when we received a letter telling us when to be in Croatia to take the flight to America, I felt hopeless. We had no papers to leave Sarajevo. Every day, my mother went to the government building to try to get papers for us. But she had no luck.

Then one day, there was a huge explosion near our apartment. Both my parents were out, and I fell on the floor screaming and crying in panic. I heard glass shattering everywhere, and the screams of those dying in the streets filled my ears. All afternoon, people were cleaning the street of shoes, blood, and pieces of human flesh. Finally, my father came home—with a loaf of fresh bread—and I found out my mother was safe at the bank.

When my mother walked in, she was white as a stone, but her eyes looked hopeful. In the midst of the chaos caused by the massacre, the worker had stamped our papers. My mother would be able to accompany me to Croatia, and from there I would fly to the United States alone.

That night, we made our way to the tunnel, the only exit from Sarajevo. I was so torn between my desire to leave the war and my need to stay with my family. How could I go? How could I stay?

As we walked toward the tunnel, grenades were falling about twenty yards from us. And every time the sky lit up, I saw the misery on the face of the people in line. We were all so frightened, all so tired.

Finally, our papers were checked and we were ready to enter the tunnel. I had no time to cry, no time to think, when I said good-bye to my father. I grabbed him and clutched him. And we moved on.

The tunnel was dank and narrow and less than five feet high; even children had to stoop to walk through. Mud and water dripped from above, and the whole tunnel smelled of urine. It seemed that we walked forever. My back burned, and the wounds on my legs were painful. Some people passed out due to exhaustion or lack of air, and others would pick up the unconscious ones and carry them. A couple of times, I started crying. Then my mother would say, "Remember, Nadja! Remember your dream!"

At the end of the tunnel, we walked silently in foot-deep mud. All around us, bombs were exploding, and we knew the snipers could see us. That walk was the longest of my life. Every time a shell exploded, I turned to see if my mother were still alive. And she whispered to me, "Keep walking! Keep walking!" The grenades sounded to me like the book of my childhood slamming shut.

Two days later, I had to kiss my mother good-bye in Croatia and board the plane to the United States. My brother had escaped to Croatia a few weeks earlier, and he, too, would be going to America.

On September 7, 1995, I arrived in the lap of peace at the home of my host family, the Yeagers in Cincinnati. I was heartsick for my homeland and my family. But the possibilities for my future were in America.

The Yeagers have loved me, taught me, and given me a chance to live. I miss my parents terribly, still. But I have seen them several times in the summers, and I dream of a day when they can come see me in America. I am at Butler University in Indianapolis now, enjoying my life, and working hard. I do not know whether I will make America my new home, or return permanently to Sarajevo.

In America, life has been relatively easy for me. Like everyone else here, I have found myself starting to take freedom for granted. I take it for granted that I can come and go between cities without difficulty, that I am free to attend the classes of my choice, that I can walk outside my door without fear.

I can feel how easy it would be for me to fall into complacency, to take this freedom and this beautiful country for granted. But instead of just living for the easygoing present, I choose to face the past.

I choose to speak out about what happened in my country. I choose to speak out about what happens to children when intolerance is allowed to grow until it explodes.

So sometimes, instead of going out with my friends, I force myself to sit and read my war diary once more. It is painful for me to put myself in that place again. But to heal these wounds, I face them.

To make sense of my suffering—and the suffering of so many thousands of others—I take the responsibility of learning from the past. And I take the responsibility of teaching others. I speak to schoolchildren about what happens when we don't respect each other's religions. I speak to youth groups and scouting groups about what happened to children their own age in my country so few years ago. I speak to adults at seminars and organization meetings.

I am committed to helping people see their freedom as the precious gift that it is. I don't want them ever to take it for granted. By forcing myself to share my story again and again, I help others understand the real meaning of this precious freedom.

And I find that the children I speak to are anxious to hear this message. They listen and ask many interesting questions. They ask me, "Does it hurt for you to talk about this to us now? Did it hurt you to write your diary? Which did you miss more—ice cream or electricity?" And, as children, they always want to know who won the war. I tell them there were no winners. There are only losers. Everyone loses so much. And the children, especially.

But when they push me on it, which they always do, and want to know who won the war, I tell them, "If you really want to know, I will say that we are the winners. The winners are the people who survived and are still not bitter or hostile in the face of intolerance."

I ask myself sometimes why God kept me alive. Why me, when so many others died every day? To answer that question, I choose to take the responsibility of living for all those who did not. When I see a beautiful sunrise, or the waves in the ocean, when I hear a bird singing its heartsong in a tree, I pay attention.

I pay attention to life for myself. And I pay attention on behalf of the boy who lay in his mother's arms while I watched his tiny bloody shoelaces swing back as forth as she ran. I listen on behalf of the woman who was murdered in the street while I watched, while she tried to buy bread for her children. I pay attention to the beauty of this world for all the children of my land who will never again see it.

It is painful for me to remember the horrors of my childhood. But if I can help other people understand the importance of love and life, and the need to turn away from the dark natures we can all carry within, then my wounds will heal. Then the spirit that war can never destroy will live on forever.

Share Nadja's passion for a peaceful tomorrow by helping to rebuild her homeland. Contact: Our Children, Musala Street 5/1, 71000 Sarajevo, Bosnia-Herzegovina. Tel: 011-387-71-442-464. Fax: 011-387-71-531-833.

Susan Kandell 1999

Sticking Her Neck Out

ANN MEDLOCK

IN 1971, I HAD IT MADE. My husband and I were partners in a successful consulting business, we were renovating a wonderful old house in Princeton, New Jersey, we were expecting our first child together, and my son from my first marriage was making the dean's list as a day student at his prep school. There were worries about the pregnancy: I was thirty-nine and had been told there were complications that meant going into labor would be dangerous. I'd have to have a Cesarean. But I was sure we'd get through it all fine. Then everything fell apart. _____

While I was on labor watch, ready to rush to the hospital at the first contraction, my husband went missing. I couldn't talk to my best friend, the new baby's god-mother, about this disaster, because I kept getting her answering service. Where could the two of them be?

The missing persons eventually turned up together, as any soap opera watcher could have predicted. Only I was dumb enough to be astonished.

I went home to two children, growing stacks of unpaid bills, an empty bank account, a ruined business, and a world of responsibilities to face alone. The worst bills were the ones from resorts, jewelers, and dressmakers—my soon-to-be ex and my former best friend were having quite a fling, on my dime. Since I was barely able to take care of my kids, much less solve clients' problems, no consulting money was coming in to offset the bills. The house went into foreclosure, my car was towed away, and one day a county constable came to the door with papers charging me with deserting my husband. I'm standing on the porch of our house, holding our baby, reading that *I* am a deserter. It was quite a moment.

A year and a half later, I was trying to read the label on a cereal box at the A&P and realized that I couldn't see it because my eyes were too full of water. Finally I got mad. I'd been crying way too long, and I was bored and angry with myself. I had been living in darkness and I had to find some light. There had to be *someone* who knew how to do that. I thought about everyone I knew, scanning for anybody who looked strong and clear and in charge of their lives. The person who fit best was a hatha yoga teacher whose class I'd taken. I called her as soon as I got home and asked how she did it—it couldn't just be the Plow or the Salute to the Sun or any other yoga position. I'd done all that stuff and was still a basket case.

She said that she worked with an Indian teacher of a more esoteric yoga, one that involved working with sound, fasting. . . . I stopped her. I didn't care about the details; clearly it worked and I wanted to go with her the next time she saw this guy.

I showed up at his sessions for the next three years. I did the work with sound, fasted, meditated, chanted, exercised, and did all-night vigils. I didn't get into the philosophy, I never took an Indian name or wore a sari, and I didn't run off to an ashram. I just used the tools his line of yogis had created and watched my life do a 180. I got fully present in my life, seeing the beauty all around me, clear about my own worthiness and abilities—and eager to serve.

There was no rule that said service was required; it just felt like the most natural thing in the world. It began when I started getting phone calls from women saying, "You don't know me but. . . " Every one of them was looking, as I had been, for someone who seemed on top of things—and they were calling me! Most of them were newly widowed or divorced and drowning in the emotions and logistics of being alone. So I called on women who were attorneys, accountants, financial analysts, and therapists to volunteer to help. We held a meeting of something we called SOLO, and more than 100 women came out on a bitter night of freezing rain. The need was clearly enormous. I worked with a group of women to get the operation rolling; then it became a YWCA effort.

When my older son graduated from the public high school (prep school was no longer possible) and my younger son was about to start kindergarten, I realized I was looking at a movable moment. If I were going to get out of Princeton, it had to be then or I'd feel I had to stay another thirteen years.

I was commuting to Manhattan for a part-time writing job, but that didn't work at all for a single mom. My kids only had one parent, and I wanted to spend as much time as possible with them.

Still I wasn't sure about moving back to the city. I'd lived there for a good chunk of my life, but never on my own. My ex was a born-and-bred New Yorker, so I'd felt I had a guide and protector when we'd lived there. All my friends were aghast at the idea of my leaving a beautiful, safe town like Princeton to live in big bad New York. But as a writer, my work was in communications, and the biggest communications playpen on Earth was right there, just a few miles away. I wanted to see if I could play with the big kids.

I made a bargain with God, one that I thought would probably keep me safely in Princeton. I'd go back to New York if I could find an affordable apartment with dawn windows on the west side of Central Park and if I could get my son a spot in the kindergarten at the Waldorf school. Rentals were scarce and pricey and all private schools had waiting lists, so I was pretty clearly loading the dice.

David aced his interview at the school and they offered him a place immediately. Then we walked straight across the park from the school and there was this humongous sign announcing the renovation of an old hotel into 300 apartments. I said, "All right, already," and signed a lease.

We went from thirteen rooms to three and it felt great—light and free. I took David to school and picked him up in just minutes, doing writing and editing jobs in the hours between. The high point was writing speeches for the Aga Khan. But making the rent also meant writing a lot of boring annual reports and advertising copy. The low point was a brochure for a company that made paper boxes for slaughterhouses; I'd been a vegetarian since meeting the yogi, and I was gagging over sentences about blood not running out of these fine boxes. This was a long way from my need to be of service. I had to find a better way to support us.

One day, I got a call from a cohort telling me to get down to *Quest 80* magazine; they were up to something that he said sounded just like me. It was perfect. I was to do press on the debut of the magazine's Giraffe Society, which was honoring twenty-one people for sticking their necks out for the common good. I loved working on something that fostered courage and service. It was so right for me I stayed on to run the Society.

Quest magazine went bankrupt, and I spent a year vainly trying to extract the Giraffe Society from the wreckage. It was just too good an idea to let die. I decided to start over, from scratch. I created The Giraffe Project. I hated the thought of losing all those members who'd signed on for The Giraffe Society, but they keep turning up—even now, more than two decades later. When I give speeches, people come up to me afterward and show me their Giraffe Society membership cards. I get e-mails and letters from old members, asking if the Giraffe Project is related to the Giraffe Society. Well, it sure is, though it's mutated mightily from the original. It is no longer tied to a commercial magazine—it's independent and nonprofit.

I started out asking people to tell me about people they knew who were sticking their necks out for the common good. I recorded interviews with these "Giraffes," wrote scripts, and chased movie stars around to record them. LPs of the stories then went in the mail to hundreds of radio stations, including Armed Forces Radio and a 500-watt station at the north pole.

Today, the Giraffe Project's headquarters are on Whidbey Island in Washington state. I'm president and the executive director is John Graham, an extraordinary man whom I married in New York sixteen years ago. Working with a staff of seven, we give Giraffe stories to editors, broadcasters, producers, and authors around the world, and produce the Giraffe Heroes Program, a K–12 curriculum based on the more than 900 Giraffe stories in our files. Schools in forty-six states are using the Program, and the Project runs a busy Web site at **www.giraffe.org/giraffe/.**

The program for schools is particularly exciting to me. It's a way to leverage my own need to serve by calling the next generations to see service as an exciting, satisfying part of their lives. And kids are responding enthusiastically. They are so much more than the consumers our commercial culture wants to make of them; they're fine, active young "citizens," eager to contribute, the way all Giraffes do.

The stories of Giraffes are personally nourishing to me, just as I hope they are to the people who read and hear them. How can you not be inspired by people like Hazel Wolf, who started agitating for the common good in 1912 and is still going—and still one of the funniest people you'll ever meet—as she approaches her 101st birthday?

Looking at now, looking at then, looking ahead to the possibilities of my own hundredth year, I am deeply grateful for the bad old days. I was not in the right place, doing the right things, with the right partner. If those times had been any less awful, if there'd been any glimmer of light in that darkness, I would have stayed stuck, unable to regroup and rebound. Now I have it all: a strong marriage, happy sons, and deeply satisfying, meaningful work. Do I forgive my ex and my errant best friend? I thank them for helping me move on to a life I couldn't have imagined way back then. There's a sign over my desk that says, "Some blessings wear a hell of a disguise." I no longer doubt that, no matter what I'm looking at.

Know of someone who is sticking his or her neck out for the common good? The Giraffe Project wants to know about it! Want to introduce the Giraffe curriculum in your school? Want to know what other Giraffes are doing? Contact: The Giraffe Project, P. O. Box 759, 197 Second Street, Langley, Washington 98260. Tel: 360-221-7989. Fax: 360-221-7817. E-mail: office@giraffe.org. Web site: **www.giraffe.org.**

Susan Kandell 1999

Bradley Artson and son

Living in the Moment

BRADLEY ARTSON

WHEN MY WIFE ELANA BECAME PREGNANT, we were delighted. We had been married for quite some time, and having children had always been a high priority. So when it looked like it was finally going to happen, we were absolutely thrilled. We were also surprised—because we found out we were going to have two at once.

Our lives as parents have turned out very differently than we had planned. Our family doesn't look on the outside like the family we had imagined. But what I've learned from our children is that there are many different ways of being in this world. And the simplest can sometimes be the best. _____

Pregnancies involving twins are always high risk, and Elana's was no exception. She started having contractions fairly early on in the pregnancy, in addition to developing diabetes. So Elana was bedridden the whole time. I had to prepare six meals a day for her—meals with very specific ingredients that had to be eaten at very specific times of the day.

That in itself was almost a full-time job. But in addition, I was a rabbi at Congregation Elat in Mission Viejo, California. I felt tremendous pressure to take care of Elana and meet my congregation's needs at the same time. My congregants were wonderful, though. People came over to cook for Elana, take her to the doctor, just do whatever was necessary. We couldn't have made it without them.

Toward the end of the pregnancy, Elana was hospitalized for two and a half weeks, and I spent every night in the hospital with her. One day, the doctors decided to check on the condition of the fetuses by doing an amniocentesis. But while doing the procedure, the doctor pierced a blood vessel. At that point, Elana had to have an emergency C-section. They whisked her out, prepped her, and put her under anesthesia. Then I watched them take my children out.

At four pounds, my daughter Shira was a giant. Little Jacob weighed only two pounds. He was so small that I could put his head in my hand and his tush would barely extend beyond my wrist. Shira stayed in the neonatal intensive care unit for about two weeks. Jacob stayed for one month. Elana spent almost all of her time at the hospital, and I spent as much time there as I could.

When both kids were finally home, they were hooked up to apnea monitors that would alert us if they stopped breathing, a real concern with premature babies. It was a scary time for us. Several times each night, those machines would make a loud beeping noise, and Elana and I would run into the babies' room with our own hearts pounding. Thank God, it was never anything serious. But the tension and worry was with us all the time.

The children did fine, though, and the next two years were a whirlwind of feeding, changing, cleaning, and other baby chores. We loved them, we cuddled them, we kissed them, and we were constantly thankful for their existence. And we were exhausted.

When the kids were about two and a half, Elana told me she felt she was losing Jacob—like she was suddenly not connecting to him. I didn't see that at all. Jacob and I have always been connected at the soul. We have an intuitive knowledge of each other that doesn't need any words. So I kept insisting to Elana that I felt the same connection with Jacob I had always had. She suggested having him tested, but I didn't really think it was necessary.

Then came the Thanksgiving preschool play. It was one of the worst days of my life. All the other children were singing and acting and dancing just like the teacher had told them, just like they had rehearsed.

But Jacob would not get out of his chair at the side of the stage. He kept rubbing his fingers in front of his eyes, fluttering his fingers. We knew something was very wrong.

When we took Jacob in for a diagnosis, the doctor administered a very brief test. Then he began to talk about autism. For reasons no one really knows, autistic children retreat, to a greater or lesser extent, into their own private worlds, usually around age two. That's what Elana had sensed from Jacob. All we have done since the day of Jacob's diagnosis is organize our lives around fighting Jacob's autism and trying to bring him out.

Autism is frustrating because so little is known about it. Just fifteen years ago, it was still considered a psychological issue brought on by bad parenting. Now it's recognized as a neurological, and possibly a viral, disorder. But there are no medications that have been proven effective, so every doctor has his or her own theory about how to treat it.

Parents of autistic kids are groping their way in the dark, desperately trying to find some way to help their child while the clock is ticking away. The general belief is that you only have until about age seven to get your child back on track. Most doctors believe it's too late after that.

Since Jacob's diagnosis, we've been through an endless series of doctors, programs, and medications—all trying to bring Jacob back into this world. Some programs have seemed to help him become more communicative and take more initiative. And others, even some that are touted in the press as the latest and greatest, have set him back for months at a time. We never really know what to expect, or even what to attribute his progress and regress to.

Predictably, Jacob's autism put a great strain on our family. Elana took leave from her job as a federal prosecutor to attend to Jacob full-time and manage his various programs. When I was offered a position as Vice President of the University of Judaism and Dean of its Ziegler School of Rabbinic Studies, Elana and I decided it would be a good move.

Like other couples who live with a stressful condition at home, Elana and I have at times found it difficult to find energy for each other, to nourish our own relationship, and focus on our own needs and desires. And, of course, Shira has a life, too. We want her to have every bit of love and attention possible. She is a joy. And, although she's definitely a typical six-year-old—which is exactly what we want her to be—she also is growing up to be a wonderful big sister to Jacob.

But what's happened to our family since Jacob's diagnosis goes much deeper than our jobs, our schedule, and our stresses. The truth is that my son Jacob has become my soul's best teacher.

Jacob was ready to teach me from the beginning, but it took me a while to hear his lessons. I was too busy struggling at first. I was too busy trying to get Jacob to fit into the life I had prepared for him. Although I hadn't realized it at the time, I had developed an entire life for Jacob before he was born. He would be bright, he would be curious, he would excel in ways that were visible to the people who mattered to me. He would be a special child.

And special he certainly is. But this is a special child who came onto this earth with his own lessons to teach, much greater in scope than those I had imagined. I have finally begun to learn.

Most recently, Jacob has taught me the true meaning of Shabbat, the Jewish sabbath. Every Saturday morning, Jacob and I would take a long walk to the synagogue. I was always very concerned about getting there on time. So I continually tried to hurry him along.

"Come on, Jacob, let's go. Let's go." That was my traditional Sabbath message to my son.

But Jacob is the king of living in the present. So he was always walking leisurely and slowly. My pushing him and hassling him did nothing but put a knot in my own stomach. By the time we got to the synagogue, I was a wreck.

Finally, one Shabbat not too long ago, I decided that instead of hassling him, I would bring a religious book and walk slowly while I read the book. I decided I would wait for him to catch up at each corner and not rush him no matter how long it took. Whenever we got there, we got there.

That was the most spiritual Shabbat I ever had in my life. And I've done that every week since then. Now I get to the synagogue on a spiritual high, and Jacob and I have a ball sitting in services together.

Another lesson I've learned from Jacob is the true meaning of God's unconditional love. Before Jacob came along, I lived in a world where people were involved in their jobs, their careers, and an endless striving to look good in other people's eyes. We all want so badly to be loved. But we seem to think we have to earn it by being successful in the eyes of the world.

Jacob taught me what I already knew in my heart: God loves us unconditionally. We don't have to be outwardly successful or "normal" in any way. In fact, we don't have to do anything at all to deserve that love. Just by being, God's love is available to us.

So many of us go through life looking at people and wondering, "What can I get out of that person?" We so rarely ask, "Why can I learn from that person? What can I cherish in that person? What can I enhance in that person?"

Those are questions I know how to ask now, because Jacob has taught them to me. We see people who are different or people who annoy us, and the only thing we think about is how we can remove ourselves from their presence. But what if we were to look at that person for just a minute through eyes of love? What if we were to pretend, just for a minute, to be that person's parent? Then you would see that person's deep value, their human potential. And that perspective changes everything. That is what I believe we're put on this planet for—to love each other that much.

I know that my suffering has made me very sensitive to other people and less judgmental. I'm much more aware of how hard it is to be the kind of person I want to be when I'm in the midst of suffering. And in some way, everyone is suffering. Everyone is dealing with something and, in their own way, doing the best they can.

In my current position with the Board of Rabbis of Southern California, I oversee an organization that runs chaplaincy programs in prisons, nursing homes, and hospitals. I have a special care for those who are ill and need a special effort to remain connected to humanity and to God. And I am committed to speaking out against social injustice and needless suffering in these institutions, or anywhere else I come across it.

Jacob has taught me to be very willing to live with vulnerability and with the awareness that all of us are ephemeral. The point is, to a great extent, to live like Jacob lives—to cherish every moment for what it is, to feel every moment for what it is.

My counseling and my teaching as a rabbi have changed since Jacob has been my teacher. I find that I am able to help people in new ways. When I talk to people about God, and His relationship to our lives, I am talking about a God Jacob has helped me see. I no longer see God as a judgmental cop giving out tickets to people who go astray. The God I speak about now is the most loving parent we could imagine. His love is always there for us. And that message is now what I as a rabbi am fully able to share with people.

I don't know what Jacob's future will bring. I don't know what anyone's future will bring. But I do know he will have a family who tries their best to help him be everything he can be. And a family who tries their best to let him teach us to be the best people we can be. I can't imagine my life now without having learned that lesson—from Jacob.

Share Brad's compassion. Help promote lifelong access and opportunities for persons within the autism spectrum and their families. Contact: Autism Society of America, 7910 Woodmont Avenue, Suite 650, Bethesda, Maryland 20814-3015. Tel: 301-657-0881. Web site: **www.autism-society.org.**

Susan Kandell 1999

Feeling Better Than Ever

Michael Mallory

I F SOMEONE HEARD BRIEFLY ABOUT MY LIFE—someone who didn't know me very well—he or she would probably say that the biggest issue in my life is the fact that I am HIV-positive. People kind of latch onto that label because it's relatively easy for them to understand. They immediately have an idea of the medical issues I'm facing and of my short-term and long-term concerns. But HIV and AIDS have never been my primary concerns.

My real issue—the issue that has caused me inner turmoil since the fifth grade—has been the reconciliation of my religious beliefs with the fact that I am gay. Everything I was taught growing up, and everything I believed, told me that what I was feeling inside was wrong and sinful. It was a long and winding road to finally be able to accept God's love just the way I am. But now, at twenty-four, I can accept myself for who I am—and I am finally able to reach out and help other people. _____

My family moved around a lot when I was young. And I mean a lot. When my father was working, he was in construction, so we moved around depending on where the work was. And even when both parents were working, sometimes they came home very late. I have a younger brother and sister, and I was pretty much responsible for the three of us. We were definitely "latchkey" kids. But I never really felt like I had it real tough—that was just the way my life was.

By the time I was eighteen, I had lived in California, Oklahoma, Texas, Mississippi, Washington, and Oregon. Sometimes I spent a whole school year in the same school. Other times, I would spend two months in one place and then move. Sometimes I would be backtracking academically, and sometimes I would be skipping ahead. I never really knew what was up from one month to the next.

It was almost impossible to make and keep friends in that situation. Everyone would like me when I first came to a new school because I was the new guy, and the new guy was always interesting. So that helped for a while. And as I got older, I tried to get involved in after-school activities right away to make friends. But in the back of my mind, I always knew I might have to leave at a moment's notice.

By the time I was a junior in high school, I decided I couldn't take moving around all the time. I was living with my father in Washington that year—my parents were separated by then—and we got into a huge fight. I ended up running away. I knew I had relatives I could live with in Bakersfield, California, but didn't want to leave in the middle of the school year. So I moved in with a friend and her family for six months, just to finish out the year.

I loved that family more than anything. They were like one of those families you see in the movies. They were nice to each other; they would talk to me about my problems. And the father would do extracurricular things with us, like take us golfing. Those six months were really happy times for me.

I also lived on and off during those years with my grandmother, my mom's mom. Grandma was a tremendous influence in my life. If there's ever been one stable force, one person whose love I needed and whom I really wanted to please, it was Grandma. She took me in many times when I had nowhere to go. And she raised me as best as she could. She taught me manners. She taught me how to be an achiever.

Grandma is a Christian woman, and she's the one who made sure I went to church. I guess she was really my moral teacher. She helped me learn about the Bible and about God. Based on her influence, I would join the Christian youth groups in all the various cities I lived in. And that was always a stabilizing factor for me.

But by the fifth grade, what I was learning in church was starting to make me uncomfortable inside. That's because even before I could consciously admit it to myself, I knew I was different. As young as I was, I felt attracted to boys.

I knew I was supposed to start being attracted to girls, but I really never felt that. Not then, not ever. What I did feel was a huge attraction to some of my male friends. I had one best friend for a while, and we did everything together. We played sports, we talked, we spent the night at each other's houses. I had a huge crush on him. And there were other guys, too, guys I would meet at school or in youth groups, or just friends of friends.

It took me years to admit to myself what I was really feeling. But deep down inside, I already knew.

Outwardly, things looked fine. I went to church and church retreats. I studied the Bible. I helped organize youth group projects and Christian clubs on campus, and I attended national Christian youth conferences.

But deep inside, I believed I was a sinner. And I absolutely could not reconcile my sexual feelings with my yearning for God's love and blessing. I suffered and struggled terribly through those years. I used to pray for God to change me, to heal me from what I saw as the affliction of homosexuality. I would continually ask God for forgiveness, and ask Him to "cure" me and make me normal.

Eventually, I felt that the only way I could go on was to accept myself like I was—and learn to be comfortable with myself as a gay person. To me, that meant I could no longer be a Christian. I loved God, and being a Christian was a very big part of my life. But I knew I couldn't stay in the church.

So by the time I started college, I was in constant inner turmoil, and my sense of self-worth was close to rock-bottom. I couldn't really see that what I did with my life was going to make much difference. I had lots of relationships with guys during those years. A few were long-term, serious, caring relationships, but most weren't. I did drugs for a while, and I drank for a while. None of it seemed to matter all that much.

Eventually, through a series of poor choices on my part, combined with just plain bad luck, I ended up on the streets of Los Angeles on New Year's Day 1997, with no money and nowhere to go. I walked the streets for the first few days of that year, going from friend to friend to ask for a meal or a place to sleep.

Finally, early one morning in January—it was a rainy morning, the first Sunday of the year—I went to see a friend of mine named Taylor. Taylor and I had had a two-year relationship, but I had left him because he was abusive. Still, I felt I had nowhere else to turn. So I knocked on his door. I told him I needed a place to sleep, just a place to eat something and take a quick shower, and then I would be gone. He told me I could come in if I had sex with him.

I said, "Taylor, no. I don't want to have that kind of relationship with you anymore. I want to be your friend. But I won't have sex with you." And so he wouldn't let me in.

I started to cry, just standing there in the rain with that door closed in my face. I could have knocked again and said, "Yes"—but I didn't. I turned and walked away. I walked for a couple of blocks in the rain, just crying. And then I realized it was Sunday. I remembered I had heard of a neighborhood church that was built by the gay community—the Metropolitan Community Church. I decided to walk there.

When I walked in, I sat down in the back and stayed through the 9 A.M. service and the 11 A.M. service, too. I cried through both services. I was coming down off drugs, and I felt so guilty and bad about so many things in my life, I didn't know what to expect or what to think.

The reverend and the pastor noticed me sitting in the back. After services, they came up and introduced themselves. They asked if they could help me. Then one of the deacons took me across the street and bought me lunch. And right that minute—feeling their love even more than my tremendous guilt—I decided to turn my life around.

I'm still sober to this day. It was that reconnection to church that I had needed to ground my life, to give me purpose, to give me a future. Since that day, that church has been the fuel that has kept me going. It continues to give me so much support.

I had been at church for a few months when I found out I was HIV positive. The first person I turned to was a man I had seen preaching at an evening service. I was so impressed with his sermon that night, I took notes on it, and he had noticed. About a week after that service I received a card from him that said, "I really want to be like your guardian angel, and help you through whatever you need help with."

So I turned to him as soon as I found out about my status. I told him I needed some spiritual guidance. He gave me a book called *God's Promises for Your Every*

Need. It's a book you can really turn to whenever you're afraid or worried. It really gives a lot of guidance—Scripture for every feeling.

I also connected with an HIV support group. When I began to feel better physically and mentally, I started becoming actively involved with the AIDS Healthcare Foundation. I began to speak out about HIV and AIDS education to youth groups and schools. After being trained by the County of Los Angeles, I started counseling gays and straights about AIDS, safe sex, and other health issues.

Now I work at the AIDS Healthcare Foundation as the administrative assistant for government affairs. I've also worked at the Foundation's community outreach center. It's actually a coffeehouse and cafe, called the WEHO Lounge, that brings HIV information to the public.

And I've developed a youth group called Plain Rap that meets in the coffeehouse. It's one of the few places in our neighborhood where young people can meet just for fun, without drinking or drugs. It's for youth in general—some straight, some gay, some HIV-positive, some not. I'm really proud of that group. We probably get about fifteen to twenty young people a night. I've also started a group called "Staying Fit with HIV." That's a support group to help people who are HIV positive deal with health issues, especially adherence to the complex drug regimens.

I'm also involved in a youth program at church. People look up to me for information about any issues related to youth and HIV.

I'm so happy now with my relationship with the church and my relationship with God. I read the Bible differently. I realize that our world has changed so much in 2,000 years, you can't take every word of the Bible literally. So I read it from a historical perspective. And, most important, I feel God's love in my life. I know my grandma still doesn't agree with this and might be kind of disappointed that I'm gay. But she's also very proud of where I am with my life now. And she has continued to be supportive.

I believe we are all here to help ourselves and each other. And I think that all along what God wanted me to do—the mission He gave me—was to help heal other people. But at the same time, by doing all that, it's helping to heal me.

If you share Michael's dream for access to services and community aware-ness, contact: AIDS Healthcare Foundation, 6255 West Sunset Boulevard, 16th Floor, Los Angeles, California 90028. Tel: 213-860-5200. Web site: **www.aidshealth.org.** In Canada, contact Swift Current United Way, Route 35 Mobile Delivery, Swift Current, SK S9H 3X6. Tel: 306-773-4828. Fax: 306-773-5686. E-mail: commerce@t2.net.

Susan Kandell 1995

Treat the Children Well

DEBBIE DAVIS

I N 1987, I DECIDED TO MARRY A MAN NAMED WILLIAM. I realize now that I based that decision on outward appearances and on other people's testimonials. If I had taken the time to get to know William better myself, I could have avoided the pain he brought to my children and to me.

I learned a lot during the time I spent with William. Most important, I learned that parents always, always, always have to put their children first. And I learned that our children are worth fighting for—all our children, not just mine. They all deserve the best. Don't let anyone tell you differently. ———

When I met William at our church in Montgomery, Alabama, I already had three children from my first marriage. I had my son Robert, who was eleven then, and daughters Mary, five, and Vicki, one. That marriage ended in divorce because my husband became a Jehovah's Witness. His church told him he had to divorce me because I believed differently.

When I met William, I had really been struggling. I was working as a private-duty nurse, never taking any money from welfare. At our church, everyone was saying such nice things about William. He told me he was a saved man who had given his life to Christ. I thought it would be good for my children to have a father around.

When we dated, he was so kind. He told me he was in college and that he was working nights. I was working, plus going to school at night and raising three kids. I didn't have a lot of time to check out what he said.

When William and I got married, the truth came out. He wasn't in college, and he wasn't working nights or any other time. I was the sole support of the family and knew pretty soon that this marriage wasn't right. But I tried to stay in it because it was supposed to be a Christian marriage, and I was taught that it would be wrong to try to get out. And I wanted to stay, too, because William and I had a son together, Kevin, the year after we got married.

After a few years, William became verbally abusive all the time. And, as I found out later, he was much worse than that with my children.

My daughter Vicki was the first one to tell me something was wrong. When she was only three years old, she told me William had been touching her. I took her to the doctor, but he said she seemed fine. In my ignorance, I believed the doctor. He was the authority figure, and I trusted him. Lord knows I should have trusted my own baby instead. But because I trusted that doctor, it was a year and a half before someone else showed me that what Vicki had said was the truth.

During that time, while I was at work, William was teaching my son Robert, who was about fourteen at the time, that it was OK for him to beat and rape both my daughters. Robert was old enough to have had a mind of his own by that time, and he should have known better. But when an adult tells a young teenager this behavior is OK, the boy believes him.

So I had a husband who was molesting one daughter, and a son who was beating and molesting both daughters. Only Kevin was spared this misery.

I finally realized that all this was going on because my daughters told my mother about it. When we reported it to the Department of Human Resources, they blamed me. They said I was a bad mother for leaving my children alone with William. They tried to take my children away from me, saying I was an unfit mother. They accused me of abusing my son Robert. And they lied to him, telling him that I was putting him up for adoption.

William left as soon as this all came out.

The state arrested Robert on two counts of rape. He has had a bad time ever since then. At first, the state put him in a special school for young sex offenders. But the ACLU filed a lawsuit because the officials there were molesting the children. So the place got shut down. Then he got into a lot of fights, and they put him back in the youth facility in Montgomery.

The sad thing is that Robert still doesn't admit to what he did. And he's mad at me because I had to focus all my attention on my girls. I had to work hard to try to get them stable again. But if I had to do it over, I would have spent more time and concern on Robert, too.

The girls and I were in terrible shape when all this came out. I couldn't do my job properly and finally had to quit. But I didn't apply for welfare. I wouldn't take a penny from the state because of what they had done to me and my family.

I just kind of withdrew into a shell. I couldn't eat, I couldn't sleep. I wanted to kill myself. My hair fell out until I was completely bald on the top of my head. And I picked at my face all the time until I had to wear makeup to hide the sores.

And the girls—oh, Lord. They were in elementary school at the time. They both started wetting the bed. And they were so scared all the time. When I would tell them to go to bed at night, Mary would cry and beg.

"Oh, Mama, I want to stay with you in your room," she would say to me. "Don't make me go in my room. Don't make me go in there in the dark. They'll hurt me in there." Mary started fighting boys at school. Even if a boy just walked by and didn't hurt her or touch her in any way, she would start fighting.

Vicki turned all her pain inside. She would sit at the table and stare straight ahead, picking the hairs out of her head one at a time. She pulled the hairs out of her eyebrows with her fingers, too, until she didn't have any eyebrows left.

A lot of people told me I should sue the system for what they did to us. And I was certainly angry enough to sue. But that's not what I wanted. I couldn't really see anything productive coming out of a fight.

What I wanted to do was improve the system so that nothing like this would happen to another family again. I wanted to teach the state what they could do to really help families. I didn't want our family's tragedy to be a negative factor for the rest of my life. Even with all I had been through, I knew God had a plan for me. And I was right.

For a while, I went to a support group, thinking it would show me what to do. I sat there and listened to people telling their stories. And I knew that wasn't a way for me to move past the pain.

Then one night I went to a meeting of the Alabama Parents' Support Network. That's when I came alive again. These parents were talking about how they could do something to change the system so that no one would have to go through this again.

I sat in that meeting and cried that night. I said, "Lord, I did not even know this kind of help existed. Thank you, Lord, for bringing me to this place." Soon I became president of the local Network group.

The first thing I did was to start more support groups to teach people about their rights as they went through the system. I taught people that the state could not just come and take away their children. There were policies and procedures that had to be followed. The state was treating these people like criminals—I knew that firsthand. But that wasn't legal. I made sure people understood their rights.

In addition, I saw there was a need for a different kind of help for families in this situation. So in 1993, I created F.A.C.E.S., which stands for Family, Advocacy, Community, Educational Services—and we do every bit of that.

When a family comes to us with a problem they're having with the social services or legal system, we take them under our wing and we walk with them every step of the way. We make sure they get fair treatment from every state agency they deal with. We help them understand the family court system. We do whatever is needed.

One family came to us because a mother couldn't get food for her children. She had fallen through the cracks, and her kids were hungry. We got them food. Another mother came in because her children had no place to sleep. We found them shelter and found a furniture store to donate mattresses.

One woman called us to say that her husband had killed her baby. But the state was charging this woman with the crime, even though she had been at work at the time. We were able to find a lawyer for her who was willing to work pro bono. And we explained to her how the system worked.

Every time I turn around, I see another need that isn't being taken care of, and so I step up and try to fix it. Now, for example, F.A.C.E.S. has a back-to-school program that gets school supplies and clothes for kids. We have summer programs for kids who have never been part of a recreation program. We work with the Air Force on a Civil Air Patrol program that keeps kids out of trouble and teaches them life skills. We have computer labs, after-school programs, career workshops, medical referral services, and mentoring and apprenticeship programs.

In the last few years, we have grown into an organization with 200 volunteers that can help 850 families a year. I appreciate all our volunteers and how much they give of their time and compassion. But I have to say that I do have two favorites—my daughters Mary and Vicki.

Mary is the president of the youth advocate group that goes to the state legislature every year to lobby for better service and laws, and she is in the Civil Air Patrol program, too. Vicki answers the phone and packs food baskets for our families.

And sometimes, in addition to speaking before the legislature, the girls share their own stories with families that come to us for help. These families feel so hopeful when they see my daughters. My girls are role models now. They were so traumatized, but now they look forward to their future.

And even though I wish with all my heart it never happened, I can see something positive that came out of our trauma. It allowed me to become a better mom and to show others how to be a better mom. Now I can tell others how important, really important, it is to listen carefully and deeply to your children.

Listen to them, protect them, and love them above all else. That's what I've learned. And that's what I'm trying to teach.

Join Debbie by reaching out to change the face of how all children are treated. Contact: F.A.C.E.S., 657 Watts Street, Montgomery, Alabama 36104. E-mail: faces@bellsouth.net. Tel: 334-613-0991. Fax: 334-286-3912. In Canada, contact Advocates for Community Based Training and Education for Women (ACTEW), 401 Richmond Street West, Suite 355, Toronto, Ontario, M5V 3A8. Tel: 416-599-3590. Fax: 416-599-2043. E-mail: actew@web.net.

Hal Ambrose Washington 1998

A Smile on His Face

JOSÉ VILLEGAS

I WAS A HAPPY, OUTGOING CHILD GROWING UP on Negros Island in the Philippines. I was a good student with a big, wonderful family and lots of friends. In college, I finished a degree in marine engineering and started studying chemical engineering. But in 1981, while I was home during summer vacation, my mother noticed a small lump underneath my chin. The local doctors removed the tumor from my chin and replaced it with bone from my hip in a bone-grafting procedure. It took months for me to recover. By then, I had missed too much school to return. So I decided to go to Manila to find a job.

After I moved to Manila, I was shocked to discover that the tumor under my chin was growing back very fast. And it grew and grew. Within two years, it weighed two pounds and hung down all the way from my chin to my chest. When I turned my head right or left, it hit my shoulders. I thought I was the ugliest person alive. For years, I rarely left my home in daylight; not even my family knew my true condition. My tumor took over my life.

Because of the tumor, I wasn't able to get a job. I was offered an overseas position at one point and had all my papers ready. But the company physicians told me they couldn't hire me because of my deformity.

I was ashamed to tell my family the truth about my situation. In the small village where I grew up, people have expectations of you when you move to the big city. Most important, they expect you to be successful. I especially didn't want to burden my mother and five sisters with my problems. I didn't want to hurt them.

So I lied and told my family I was OK, but that I just wanted to stay in Manila. They sent me some money, and I rented a small room. I started doing odd jobs just to survive. I hid my situation for almost three years. They didn't think it was unusual that I didn't come home for a visit, because they knew it was a twenty-two-hour boat ride from Manila to Negros Island.

I did go see doctors in Manila. Even though I had lost faith in doctors after my first surgery, I knew I needed help. But every doctor I saw described a different scary procedure. One even said he would remove my lower jaw, stretch the skin from my chin to my chest, and leave it there for several months. I didn't have the surgery.

Another doctor did a biopsy. I developed a serious infection and almost died. For two and a half years, I had to change bandages twelve to fifteen times a day because of that infection. It was terrible.

I was confused and scared. And after a while, I stopped going out, because people would just stare at me. When I absolutely had to go out—to the post office, for example—I took a jeepney. A jeepney is like a small bus where people sit facing each other. I would wear a bandana over my chin to try to hide the tumor. But still, I would never look up at anyone on the jeepney. I would just look down the whole time.

One day, I met a mother with a one-year-old son in a grocery store. In the course of our conversation, I touched the boy's shoulder. Later that night, the mother searched me out.

"What did you do to my son?" she demanded. "My boy has stomach cramps now. You put a spell on him when you touched him!" And she told me she needed some of my saliva to remove the spell. It was such a horrible moment. I would never do anything to hurt a child—any child. I felt frustrated and ashamed. I really didn't know how I could go on.

Then, in 1984, an old acquaintance of mine invited me to a Bible study group. That's where I first heard that if you give your heart to God, He will give you peace that surpasses all understanding. And that's what I did. I asked God for guidance. And I told Him I would believe in Him, no matter what happened with my tumor or any other part of my life. And the truth is that from that day on, my life was changed. I still had my tumor, but my burden felt so much lighter. And I was very grateful.

About a year and a half later, someone knocked on the door to my room to tell me my mother was downstairs. I was shocked. I didn't want her to see me the way I was. But one of my town mates had told my parents about my situation, and my mother had immediately taken a boat to Manila. She had never been that far from home before, but she rushed to see me as soon as she heard. I was touched by that.

So I went downstairs to see her, afraid of what her reaction would be.

"You don't look bad. You look OK to me, José," she said. "I want you to come home." It was a simple statement—but one that meant everything in the world to me.

I told my mother she should go home first, and I would decide what to do. I still had my pride. A girlfriend from years earlier still lived in my hometown, and I didn't want her to see me like this. I felt so ugly and like such a failure. But I thought and I prayed about it. And the next year, I did go home to my island.

People were very kind and accepting, and they wanted to know what I had been through. I will never forget their kindness.

In February 1987, I went back to Manila because I knew the Operation Smile doctors would be there. I had learned about Operation Smile—an organization of volunteer doctors who perform surgery all over the world—on a Christian television show, and I wanted to see if the doctors could help me. The day of the screening, I was shocked to see hundreds of other people with tumors and deformities, waiting to see the doctors.

The doctors could not operate on everyone, because there wasn't enough time. So they had to screen the patients and choose who would receive the surgery. I saw young children turned away. I knew that getting the surgery at a young age could make a big difference in a child's life. It could prevent that child from having to go through what I went through.

I went back to see Operation Smile's doctors three years in a row—1985, 1986, 1987. Those first two years, I was put on the waiting list.

In 1987, when I made my third trip to see Operation Smile, I was very, very sick. I weighed only 99 pounds. I was dying. I had been praying for three years for the right doctor to operate on me. As soon as I met the doctor, I knew he was the right doctor for me. He held my hand and looked me in the eyes. And he said something I never expected to hear.

"José, I hear you play the guitar," he said to me. "I was wondering if you could teach me how to play. It's something I've always wanted to learn."

Just like that, this man was treating me like a normal person. He was asking *me* to help *him*—something no one had asked of me in so long. He had such compassion, and I trusted him.

But, as badly as I wanted him to help me, I couldn't forget that other children were waiting for help. I didn't want a young child to end up suffering as I had. So, when I was finally selected for surgery that year, I gave up my spot so that a child could have the surgery instead. I knew it was the right thing to do.

Operation Smile didn't let me down that year. They made me their Number 1 priority for treatment in the United States.

In July 1987, Operation Smile brought me to the United States for my surgery. On July 30, I had the surgery. And on July 31, my birthday, I woke up without the tumor. I had a great, great gift from God for my birthday—a new look.

It took a total of nine surgeries over four years to completely repair my jaw. I stayed mostly in the United States during those years; by 1991, the surgeries were finished.

During those years, I started working for Operation Smile. The first thing I did was to care for thirteen young patients who had come from Africa. The nanny Operation Smile had hired for them resigned after two weeks, and they asked me to step in. I loved taking care of them. I could relate to the patients, and I loved giving back what Operation Smile gave to me. After that, I wrote a song for Operation Smile. By 1990, I was working for them full-time.

For three years, I worked as the Operation Smile warehouse manager. I learned how to identify all the surgical supplies and equipment that was to be used on each of the missions to different countries.

These days, I am the Speakers Bureau coordinator for Operation Smile. I work with fifty-three volunteer speakers nationwide. Each of these people has been on an Operation Smile mission and has a story to tell. It's my job to match them up with groups all over the country who want to learn more about the organization.

I've had a chance to go with the team on one mission a year. Last year, I went to Colombia. Each trip is about eleven days including travel, with three full days of screening and five of surgery. Those trips are so wonderful. I see that all around the world, mothers have the same love for their children. You can see it in their eyes. And now that I have been blessed with a wonderful wife and a new baby boy, I can fully understand these parents' compassion and pain.

When I lived in Manila as a young man in my twenties, afraid to show my face in the light of day, who would have thought I would one day have the full and beautiful life I have now?

And so, although I never would have imagined I would feel this way, I am thankful for that terrible period of my life. If I had not had that experience, I would not be the grateful person I am today. Now the memory of my own pain motivates me and helps me to really make a difference in other people's lives.

If you know of a child who lives in the United States and who suffers from a facial deformity, or if you would like to get involved domestically, please contact: Operation Smile, 6435 Tidewater Drive, Norfolk, Virginia 23509. Tel: 877-SMILE50 (Domestic Medical Program) or 757-321-SMILE (Operation Smile Headquarters). Fax: 757-321-7660. Web site: **www.operationsmile.org.**

A Guide to Freedom

BO LOZOFF

L IKE SO MANY OTHER YOUNG PEOPLE IN OUR CULTURE, I grew up without any real sense of direction, without any connection to a purpose greater than myself. I went where I went and did what I did without putting any real thought into those decisions.

I can't regret that part of my life, though, because the lessons I learned from those paths converged to bring me to a turning point in 1972. That's when I met Ram Dass, the man who showed me by example what it means to lead a spiritual life. It was then that my wife and I began to meditate, practice yoga, and change our focus to one of service. And it was through Ram Dass that we ultimately undertook the responsibility to help men and women in prison with their spiritual and emotional growth. Since that time, I guess we have helped quite a few people turn their lives around. But the truth is, they've helped us much more. _____

I was left on my own pretty much as a child. I don't mean that I was alone on the streets of Miami, where we lived, I just mean I didn't get a lot of guidance from my family. When I was eight years old, my father had a massive stroke that left him paralyzed. When that happened, the family went into survival mode, putting a lot of energy into taking care of my father and meeting his needs. There just wasn't much energy left over to take care of four children, of whom I was the youngest.

I was pretty much left to finish growing up on my own. And I didn't do a very good job of it. By the time I started into adolescence, I was morose and brooding. I felt ashamed and embarrassed to have a crippled father. And then I felt guilty about being ashamed and embarrassed. I worried a lot. I had a lot of angst. I didn't have any friends, didn't talk a lot, didn't socialize much.

But I did spend a lot of time thinking and reading. And I have never forgotten one very important passage that I read during that time. In a way, it foreshadowed so much of what my life was to become.

I was reading *The Prophet* by Kahlil Gibran. And what he had to say about crime and punishment jumped out at me. He said that the highest that is in the highest saint is in you, and the lowest that is in the lowest murderer is also in you. As a kid, that concept led me to a very deep understanding that everyone really has the same range of possible emotions and actions. We're all much more similar than we might seem.

I spent my adolescence bouncing from one thing to the next—trying to find my place in this world. I had no real sense of myself, no goals, no purpose. I did bodybuilding for a while, entered college at sixteen, and attempted suicide the week of my eighteenth birthday. By the time most kids my age were graduating high school, I was back in Miami after having been kicked out of college, with absolutely no idea of what I was going to do.

Then one day in 1966, the year after I went back home, I was running an errand for my brother, when I saw a beautiful young woman unloading groceries from her car. I pulled my car over, grabbed two grocery bags she had left on the trunk of her car, and followed her to her doorway.

She was startled and scared, so I put her groceries down and left. But a few months later I saw her again, and we got into a deep conversation about the fact that there had to be something deeper and truer than the self-centeredness, racism, and greed we saw all around us. And right then and there we pledged to look together for whatever that truth was. That very night, I moved in with her. A few months later, Sita and I were married.

Right about that time, my oldest brother was beginning to get involved in the civil rights movement. And through him, Sita and I became involved for the first time in political activism. We began working to help organize farmworkers in Florida.

The situation with the farm workers was ugly and violent. Their living conditions were horrible, and the relationship between the farmers and the workers were shameful. It wasn't a pleasant place to be, but for the first time in our lives, we felt devoted to a cause that we knew really meant something.

After working actively in the violence and tension of civil rights for a couple of years, Sita and I opened the first head shop in Atlanta in 1968, trying sincerely (if naively) to bring the "flower-power" culture of nonviolence into the deep South. Instead, it turned out to be a very violent time.

It was open season on hippies in Georgia in those days, and I can't even count the number of times I was arrested. Once I found myself drawing a gun on the Atlanta police. I shot at some neo-Nazis who were trying to kill us. It was craziness. Finally, when it became clear that the police were going to put me in prison or kill me, Sita and I gave up and left.

By 1969, we felt lost. We had no home, no interests, and no money. We were burned out on activism and politics. We literally just wanted to sail away into the sunset and drop out. So we hired on as first mate and cook with my brother-in-law and a man who was leaving Florida to sail around the world on a boat he had built.

Things went well for a few months. But then the boat owner, who knew my brother-in-law was a drug dealer, decided to make some quick money. Since Sita and I didn't want to risk getting involved with the police again, we got off the boat in Jamaica before the drugs were loaded on. Everyone involved with that deal got busted. My brother-in-law was sentenced to twelve to forty years without parole.

Sita and I, who were becoming very interested in Eastern philosophy, landed in North Carolina, where I got a job in the Duke University parapsychology lab. As part of my job, I visited various swamis who had come over from India to see if we could interest them in working in a laboratory setting. It was at that time that I met Ram Dass, the author of *Be Here Now*. Ram Dass and I felt an immediate connection, and after working with him, Sita and I opened a small ashram, a quiet, secluded place to focus on meditation and yoga.

For the next few years, we did a lot of meditation and yoga. And every time we would visit my brother-in-law in prison, we became more aware that prisoners could benefit from these practices. If I didn't try to reach out to them, who would?

So I started meeting with people in prison administration and talking about teaching meditation and yoga. Right around that time, Ram Dass had also begun to work with prisoners, sending *Be Here Now* to prison libraries around the country. He was getting so much correspondence from the prisoners that he just didn't have time to handle all the mail. He asked me if I would take that over.

And that was the beginning of the Prison Ashram Project. We had no idea this would become our life's work. It just seemed right at the time.

The Prison Ashram Project has grown to something we had never envisioned. In the 1980s, it became so big that Sita and I founded the Human Kindness Foundation as a nonprofit organization to sponsor the project.

We now have a mailing list of almost 40,000 people. We send our books and tapes at no charge to prisoners or people who work in prison, and I've conducted workshops in more than 500 prisons all around the world.

But Sita and I don't feel that we've ever led this work. We feel we have been following it. This work has been our guru. And the work has gradually changed us over the past twenty-five years.

For example, I've gone into many prisons to discuss meditation and bringing a sense of spiritual peace into your life. But suppose that I myself couldn't meditate unless I had a special meditation room with a beautiful bowl of flowers and just the right incense burning? Or suppose that I thought I couldn't lead a spiritually correct life unless I ate only sugar-free organic granola?

If that's where I was coming from, how could I possibly talk about meditation to a man who is locked up in a cell twenty-four hours a day, seven days a week, with absolutely nothing in his room—not even a mattress—except a hole in the floor to defecate into?

So what Sita and I learned from the Prison Ashram Project is that we needed to simply our own lives—simplify our beliefs, our practices, our surroundings.

Sita and I have a guru from the Hindu tradition. But since not many people in this country relate to Hinduism, we have refined our own beliefs and what we've learned from our work into three main principles that we see reflected in every one of the world's major religions. So whether a person's background is Christian, Muslim, Jewish, Buddhist, or Hindu, everyone can understand their relevance.

The three principles we teach in our work are simple living, spiritual practice, and unselfish service.

Those principles are the core of what we have learned from our twenty-five years of working with prisoners. They are the foundation of how we live our own lives, and they are the foundation of what we teach. If everyone lived simply, did some kind of prayer or meditation every day, and dedicated themselves to helping others, we would have a wonderful world to live in.

Sita and I don't feel that the prisoners we work with are very different from ourselves. Just like the passage from *The Prophet* that I read as a teenager, I've learned that we all have the same possibilities within us. I could have so easily killed someone when I fought my battles with the Atlanta police. So I understand perfectly how that can happen. And I have known thousands of people who have raped, killed, or attacked others. But every spiritual tradition teaches us that those people are as worthy of eating at the Father's table as the rest of us. After all, Jesus took Saul of Tarsus, a man who had arrested, tortured, and killed people, and turned him into Saint Paul.

So we accept all kinds of people in the Prison Ashram Project and at our Kindness House, the spiritual community that is the headquarters for Human Kindness Foundation. We accept people who come here to learn about these three principles, people who want to move forward from wherever they have been.

While we accept people no matter what they've done, I must admit I don't personally relate to the popular issue of forgiveness. It sounds like maybe what you did turned out to be all right. Is it ever all right to have blown another person's head off in anger, or molested a child? I don't trust the contemporary treatment of forgiveness, which is sort of like "Put it all behind you." Maybe for most middle-class issues like scratching the neighbor's minivan or even having an affair with a friend's spouse, the people involved can all move on past it. But you can't just put murder or rape behind you like that.

But if you accept responsibility, and learn to live by these three principles, then you can move forward. Are you forgiven? I don't know. But you can be a humble, productive person who can help others greatly. And your life can be changed. I'd rather leave the forgiveness up to God.

Few people have taught me that better than Michael, one of the men who has come to Kindness House. By the time Michael was twelve, he was living on the streets. By the time he was seventeen, he had committed enough crimes, including murder, to be put away for life. Jim was in prison for twenty-three years before he came to Kindness House, and is now one of my most valued and trustworthy staff at the Human Kindness Foundation.

The goal of our program wasn't to forgive Michael so he could get his self-esteem back and feel happy. But in the process of living simply, following spiritual practices, and selflessly helping others, he has become happy. I don't think Jim ever could have anticipated the wonderful life he is leading now.

All of us have parts of ourselves that can do terrible things. But what Sita and I have learned is that that doesn't have to define the whole person.

Yes, that part of me that did something terrible will always feel terrible. That particular cloud will always hang over me. But my sky can grow so that the frame around the cloud can become so much bigger. And then I can see my way to a life of faith and joy.

Learn more about Bo's work and/or how to become involved with the Human Kindness Foundation. Contact: Human Kindness Foundation, Route I, Box 201-N, Durham, North Carolina 27705. Tel: 919-942-2540. Fax: 919-304-3220. Web site: **www.humankindness.org/**.

Susan Kandell 1999

A True Free Spirit

SUE TURK

IF I HAD TO DESCRIBE MYSELF IN TWO WORDS, I think I would have to say *free spirit*. I've always been a person who loves to move and dance and sing. I love to perform and entertain. I love spontaneity, to go with the flow. But then I was diagnosed with diabetes—an illness that requires your attention practically twenty-four hours a day. And unless your idea of fun is giving yourself blood tests and shots, diabetes and spontaneity just don't mix well.

But now—although there was a time when I never thought I'd hear myself say this—I see my diabetes as a learning experience. It has given me a compassion for other people's pain and the gift of putting my own pain in perspective. And it has enabled me to bring joy into some young lives that I might otherwise not have been able to touch. _____

I was twenty-eight years old when I was diagnosed with diabetes, but I should have been diagnosed before that. Much earlier, I had symptoms and signs no one was paying attention to.

I had given birth to a very high birth-weight baby—almost eleven pounds. I started getting more and more fatigued from tennis games. I was thirsty all the time. I seemed to drink gallons of water, but nothing ever really quenched my thirst. And my performances in semi-professional and community theaters—which I had been doing for years—were suddenly exhausting me. That exhaustion really concerned me, because I loved the theater so much. At the time, I was the lead dancer in *Applause*, my favorite show, and I wanted to keep doing it forever.

All of the symptoms pointed to diabetes. But I didn't realize it, and none of the health care professionals I saw picked up on it either. Then my husband Mike—who is a retired vice president of AT&T—was transferred from our home in New Jersey to California, and I told him I thought I should see my doctor before we moved. I just had a feeling that something was up.

As I was leaving my doctor's office, the doctor came up to me in the hallway and said, "Sue, it looks like you have high blood sugar. You need to see a specialist."

I happened to have a cousin who had low blood sugar problems, and her doctor was nice enough to talk to me on the phone. I went over to his office, he did some tests and told me, Yes—I had diabetes. And that was the beginning of this new phase of my life.

Initially, I thought that diabetes was only going to be a small part of my life, and I could accept that. I had always been a very accepting and flexible person. So I thought I could accept this, too.

But I soon felt that diabetes had taken away my whole life.

The disease forced me to eat a very specific, restricted diet. And I had to eat exactly so much at exactly such-and-such time of the day. I had to carry a little pad of paper around with me all day and write down every single thing I ate. I had to give myself blood tests and write down my sugar levels all day long.

Then—based on what I ate, my exercise schedule, and what my blood tests showed—I had to calculate how much insulin I needed. And all of it had to be done on a strict timetable.

I hated having such a rigid routine. My free-spirit personality didn't want to go for it. And the nurse I worked with was almost as frustrated as I was. "Sue, I can't help you," she said to me one day. "I just can't help you anymore because you don't have a routine in your life."

So I tried. I really tried for a while to do things by the book. And on the outside, it looked like I was coping. I carried around my pad of paper, and I wrote things down. I gave myself the shots. I did it all like they said.

But on the inside, I was incredibly angry and frustrated. I felt like these constant restrictions were squeezing all my energy and personality into a teeny, tiny little box with a heavy, locked lid. My life just wasn't my own any more. And I resented it all day, every single day.

So I rebelled—big time. I decided to take a one-week vacation from diabetes. I still gave myself my insulin shots that week, but I threw the rest of my restrictions out the window. For a whole week, I ate anything and everything I wanted in the whole wide world. I ate sugar, sugar, sugar, and sugar, as much as I could get my hands on.

I loved it. I had such a tremendous sense of freedom. I was finally out of prison and back in control of my own life.

But, of course, there was that one small kink in my plans: My mind had gone on vacation, but my body chemistry had not. And so by the end of the week, I was rushed to the hospital very nearly in a diabetic coma with kidney, blood pressure, and cholesterol problems.

Finally, many years after my diagnosis, I came to terms with my diabetes in 1997. I had been fighting it for so long, and putting so much emotional energy into that fight, and I didn't want to do it any more. I finally figured out that I really had only two choices. I could either accept this disease, take responsibility for managing it, and live a full, rich life. Or, I could keep fighting it, ruin my health, and possibly even die.

I chose life. And once I made that decision, I felt a great sense of freedom.

When I finally came to terms with my diabetes, I chose to treat it with an insulin pump. It was a big step, because it's an invasive device—a twenty-four-hour-a-day reminder that you're a diabetic. But once I accepted this disease as a permanent part of my life, switching to the pump made a lot of sense.

The pump looks like a pager. It's small and gray and clips to my skirt, pants, or bra. The insulin is pumped continuously into my belly through a needle, which is changed every three days. It still takes a lot of work on my part to calculate everything, but I have so much more freedom in my schedule with the pump. And that's worth a lot to me.

That freedom in my schedule gives me more flexibility with the work I do now—clowning to entertain sick children.

I originally became interested in clowning when my husband Mike was a plant manager in Reading, Pennsylvania, about ten years ago. I attended a plant dinner at which clowns were performing. I spoke to several of the clowns and found out that they were part of the AT&T Pioneers, a community service organization that performs at hospitals, nursing homes, and the Special Olympics.

I loved their act so much that I knew immediately this was something I had to do. And Mike agreed. Clowning fits right in with my love of performing. And what better way is there to help people than to give them a few minutes of love and laughter?

So I became Sweet Pea, and Mike became Buttercup. We made our costumes out of old clothes, carefully designing something silly and fun that children would love. Sometimes, we spend an hour just putting on our makeup—and end up with as much powder on the floor as on our faces. But we are so happy to bring happiness to other people. It's like the old thrill of theater performance—only better.

These days, Mike and I concentrate our efforts volunteering as clowns at the Valerie Fund Center. The Valerie Fund treats thousands of children annually with cancer or blood disorders in five hospital-based centers in New Jersey. We entertain kids on the hospital floors and at holiday parties—in groups or one on one. And a lot of times, I show the kids my insulin pump. They can see it on the outside of my costume anyway. But I'm very comfortable with it, and I show them the part that goes into my belly. Whenever the kids see the pump, I always sense that they like me better than before. They realize I'm really one of them. They have machines and needles poking and prodding them. And so do I.

We do whatever it takes to bring a smile to their faces. Sometimes we sit on the floor quietly and make silly faces with them. Sometimes we make balloon animals. Sometimes we get them to giggle by squirting water on them from our lapel flowers. And in those special moments of smiles and laughter, those children forget about their pain. They forget about the tubes going in and out of their bodies. They forget about their bald heads. They're just kids—laughing at clowns, just like kids do all over the world. And we know we've done our job.

Usually, we come to the hospital to entertain a group of kids. But sometimes the hospital calls us to come down because one particular child needs some help.

I remember one patient in particular named Lasheera. Lasheera was a darling little girl with no hair, about three years old. She was getting ready to have some surgery, and she asked for us. I sat on the floor with her while she was waiting for her surgery. I made some balloons and did a little bit of magic, and she just loved the colors and the touching. It was such a wonderful experience to see her laugh and forget about her pain for a moment. Lasheera made it through that surgery, but she died a few weeks later. And when I heard of her death, I thought about the short moment she and I spent together—and how much she gave to me with her sparkling eyes and beautiful smile.

It's not always easy to walk through a cancer ward. Many of the children we clown for aren't going to make it. And we know that. It's hard to walk in laughing and joking when our hearts are breaking for these sick kids. I've cried more than once.

But we always leave grateful—counting our blessings and thanking God that our own children and grandchildren are happy and healthy. And we leave with the knowledge that we really have brightened someone's day. In fact, more than once, nurses have told us that our visit was the only time a particular child smiled that entire day. What a blessing it is to be able to do this!

In addition to working in the hospitals, Mike and I volunteer for one week every summer at the Valerie Fund's camp for children with cancer. It's called Camp Happy Times in the Pocono Mountains in Pennsylvania. We work as assistants to the director.

The camp allows these kids to forget that they have any problems. A little girl who's been hiding her bald head under a hat for three months will come to camp and an hour later the hat is gone. These kids are here to have a great time, just like kids going to camp anywhere else. And that's how we look at it, too.

We want to give them a week they'll never forget. Sometimes we clown for them, and sometimes we help them learn how to clown, too. For one week, these kids have a chance to feel normal. Mike and I look forward to Camp Happy Times so much. It's a wonderful, wonderful experience.

Our other love, besides clowning, is teaching clowning to others. We have classes where we teach a group of teenagers some of the basics for a couple of hours. And at the end of the class, we all go to a hospital and try out what we learned. The teenagers and the adults see that they can make a difference—they can bring laughter to a sick child. They leave with much more than they gave. And I know that at the end of that day, another group of sick children will have been able to forget their pain for a moment, thanks to these newly minted clowns.

I definitely see myself today as a free spirit in the true sense of that term. I realize now that being a free spirit isn't about freedom from a schedule or a routine. It's about having my own spirit uplifted by bringing happiness to others.

Share Sue's goal of providing medical care in a happy, upbeat child-centered atmosphere. Contact: The Valerie Fund, 101 Millburn Avenue, Maplewood, New Jersey 07040. Tel: 973-761-0422. Fax: 973-761-6792. Web site: **www.TheValerieFund.org.** In Canada, contact the Canadian Diabetes Association, 15 Toronto Street, Toronto, Ontario, M5C 2E3. Tel: 416-363-3373. E-mail: info@cda-nat.org.

Building Peace in a Broken World

JENNY SOLOMON

WHEN MOST CHILDREN GET STOMACHACHES, they're sick for a few days and then they get over it. This unfortunately was not the case for me. Instead, I went from stomachache to stomachache and from doctor to doctor, but no one could seem to help me. From the time I was thirteen, doctor visits and medical tests were part of my life. It wasn't easy, but it was the way things were for me.

What I've learned from my illness—what I've learned about caring for people, about healing, and about life itself—has helped shape me into the person I am today. I plan to help as many people as I can along the way. _____

In Judaism, we call an act of community service or of helping other people a *mitzvah*. Our religion teaches us that these mitzvahs—or *mitzvot*—are not optional. We are required to perform mitzvot to care for ourselves, our families, and our communities. Even before I became ill, much of my life revolved around this concept.

For as long as I can remember, mitzvot were a way of life in my home. Even as a child, I was aware that reaching out to help others formed my most intimate connections to Judaism and my Creator. As children my sister and I never received allowances. We learned that we did the dishes and cleaned our rooms because, along with the love, the hugs, and the laughter, this meant being part of a family. Our parents taught us that, even as children, we had obligations and responsibilities as family members. And even as children, our contributions made a difference.

We felt the same way about our community. Each week when my parents drove me to religious school, I made sure I had some money with me to give to charity. I can vividly recall sitting with my mother and making lists of people we would honor by making donations in their name for certain Jewish holidays. We welcomed strangers into our home on every holiday, brought food to people who could not prepare their own meals, and as a whole family discussed what special donations we wanted to make.

As I grew older, I began to take charge of my own mitzvah ideas and projects. Working as a camp counselor for developmentally disabled teenagers and young adults and as a counselor-mentor with sixth- and seventh-graders at Frederick Douglass Academy in Harlem were very rewarding experiences.

At school, I coordinated a project to prepare a meal once a month for 300 homeless people at a local shelter. I coordinated monthly birthday parties for children who had been removed from abusive homes. I became president of my school's community service organization.

But while I was working hard to help other people, I was having health problems of my own. I was often sick and in pain with stomach problems. My parents took me to doctor after doctor. I often felt like I was crazy, because no one seemed to recognize that there was something medically wrong with me.

My symptoms were painful and embarrassing—gas, bloating, distention, chronic constipation, bouts of diarrhea, esophageal reflux, bowel obstruction, and constant cramps. They were symptoms that would be difficult for anyone to deal with. But for a teenager, they were even harder. I would spend hours at a time in the bathroom. Or I would go out with friends and be cramped up and miserable the entire time.

When I was seventeen, my parents took me to the Mayo Clinic in Rochester, Minnesota. The treatments I underwent during the seven days I spent there were among the greatest challenges I have faced in my life. I fasted during the day and then drank a "potion" at night to clear my system out completely. Then I went in for a test, only to learn I would have to fast for twelve more hours and drink yet another potion.

My days there were filled with one uncomfortable, humiliating test after the next, always with foreign medical students watching for educational purposes. Just imagine trying to come up with conversation at a time like that! The best remedy I found that week was definitely humor.

At the end of that week, I got good news and bad news. On the good side, I finally found out what was wrong with me and that many of my symptoms could be controlled by diet. The bad news was that my disease was never going to go away.

I have celiac sprue, a genetic disease involving damage to the lining of the small intestine. People with this disease can have the same physical symptoms I did, plus malnutrition. To treat it, I have to stay completely away from all gluten products, including anything that contains even minimal amounts of wheat, rye, or barley. It sounds so simple, but even a gluten-free food product made by a machine that previously came in contact with gluten can make me sick, so it can be quite tricky to stay healthy.

At seventeen years old, it was difficult to comprehend that I would have a serious digestive disorder for the rest of my life. It took me a while to accept it. At first, I told myself I just wasn't going to let it get me down. I forced myself to push forward on my busy schedule. I ate some foods I knew I shouldn't have, even though I suffered for it physically. I tried to always put on a good show, because I wanted to prove to myself, and to my family and friends, that there was really nothing wrong with me.

But after a while, I knew I needed to take another look. I realized that if I wanted to feel as well as I could, I had to come to terms with the fact that this disease was a reality for me. I had to stop pretending. I had to start taking care of myself.

I learned that I could strike a balance between "giving into" my disease and pushing myself forward as if nothing were wrong. If I were really in so much pain that I had to stay in bed, then that really was the best route to go right then—and I didn't want to feel guilty about it. But I also learned that sometimes it was best for me to get out of bed and be with other people, even if I wasn't physically comfortable.

That was especially helpful to me if I were going to work on a community service project. If I were helping other people in some way, I felt so much better emotionally, even if I didn't feel great physically. At a moment when I could have been in bed feeling hopeless and useless, I instead felt that I had great purpose.

I still felt frustrated sometimes that I couldn't be like everyone else and that my friends really didn't understand my problems, but I was so excited about the many projects I was involved in helping others. I realized I could make a difference—and that became my focus.

In my senior year of high school, I was elected by my school faculty and administrators to speak at my graduation. I chose to speak about the Jewish values that formed the core of everything I believed—reaching out to others and being of service. I was nervous standing in front of my class, the Greenhill School community, and hundreds of family members and friends. I was outside the safety of my temple and summer camps, and my speech sounded more like a sermon than a typical high school graduation speech. But it was from my heart. So I held on to my vision and said what I had come to say.

"I would like to change the world and be the best person I can be," I told them. "I can't be the next Golda Meir or John F. Kennedy. I can only be Jenny. But that in itself is no small feat. I know it is not always easy to be ourselves and believe in who we are. But as the Jewish sage, Hillel, said, 'If I am not for myself, who will be for me?'" I spoke aloud the words I knew so well, the words I understood even better after coming to terms with my diagnosis.

I entered Brown University in 1993 and found an incredible group of friends who supported me. They were kind, caring, and respectful. At times, my friends would sit outside the dorm bathroom and tell people it was out of order so that I could have an hour in there by myself. I befriended the campus chefs, and they cooked meals just for me. "Why are you so lucky to get special meals?" people in the dorm would ask. I would chuckle and tell them how my stomach usually felt and ask if they wanted to trade.

In addition to finding ways to meet my own needs, I turned my energies to community service. My mitzvot focused on teaching and trying to build bridges between people of different backgrounds. This was my passion.

My ultimate teaching experience came when I was one of twelve students accepted into Brown's Urban Education Semester program. I worked as a student teacher in a second-grade classroom and took a full load of graduate courses at night. Because the area I worked in was predominately Dominican, I taught nearly half the day in Spanish. In addition, I worked privately with several students who were recent arrivals from Puerto Rico or the Dominican Republic and had no English skills at all.

It was a gift to have the opportunity to work with these children. When I looked into their eyes, I felt a mystical, magical quality. They were untouched by the hardness and prejudice of the world. Their potential for intellectual and spiritual growth was unbounded. I loved learning about them and their culture, and sharing my Jewish and American culture with them.

This extraordinary opportunity helped me realize that the mitzvah of making peace between people—of people learning about each other with dignity and respect—is the mitzvah that is dearest to my heart.

When I was not teaching, I put my energies into creating a Black-Jewish Alliance at Brown University. Our group participated in many projects and social activities, including one trip to Washington D.C. that I will never forget.

We spent the last day of that trip at the United States Holocaust Memorial Museum. By nighttime, we were emotionally drained. About eighteen of us met in one of our hotel rooms and started dancing to the music on a local contemporary black radio station. Then one girl suggested turning the radios off and learning some Israeli folk dancing. We ended up dancing for hours that night—alternating between Israeli folk dancing accompanied by our own singing and contemporary dancing to the black radio station. It was a cultural connection none of us will ever forget.

I now know that all of the mitzvah projects I have participated in, projects that looked on the surface like teaching experiences for me, were actually learning experiences. Each has been a source of healing and strength. And through all of these projects, I have learned about the direction my life must take.

I want to dedicate my life to building peace in a broken world. I am now studying to become a rabbi, as is my husband, Eric. Rabbis are not only spiritual leaders; they are teachers. They teach from the heart, as well as from the book.

I know there will still be days when I have to force myself—train myself, really—to get beyond my own physical pain. And some days that will be especially difficult. But I know that if I listen to my heart—and to the lessons I've learned from so many others—I will be able to make a difference.

Want to do a mitzvah? Any city, many ideas. Contact: Ziv Tzedakah Fund, 384 Wyoming Avenue, Millburn, New Jersey 07041. Tel: 973-763-9396. Fax: 973-275-0346. E-mail: naomike@aol.com. Web site: **www.ziv.org.**

Russ Fischella 1992

Crowning Glory

PEGGY KNIGHT

ONE NIGHT WHEN I WAS FOURTEEN YEARS OLD, I went to bed a normal teenager. But when I woke up, my life had changed. I looked in the mirror that morning as always. But instead of seeing the hair I was used to, I saw a bald spot about the size of a quarter. I was terrified and confused. And embarrassed.

That morning was the beginning of a long journey for me, although I didn't know it at the time. Alopecia areata, the autoimmune condition that caused my hair to fall out, eventually brought me to my lowest point in life. But it also opened the door for me to help other people in a way I never anticipated.

Alopecia areata can strike anyone at any time. In my case, it hit my mother and me at once. I started out with patches of hair loss that came and went, and slowly grew larger over a long period of time. But my mother's hair loss progressed very rapidly. She was completely bald about six months after she discovered her first bald spot.

I lived in fear that I would become like her. I spent hours and hours of my life every week working with my hair so that I could pretend to the outside world that I was completely normal. But nothing I did with my hair could take away my fear.

Alopecia can cause hair patterns to change constantly, so you never know what you're going to wake up with. One day, the bald spot might be on your left side, and you work and work with your hair to cover that up. But two days later, that spot might already have a covering of dark fuzz where the hair was starting to grow back. Instead, a large patch of hair directly in the front might have fallen out during the night.

So every morning, I saw a different face in the mirror. Every morning was a unique challenge. My friends got up in the morning wondering what clothes to wear. But my morning chore became: How am I going to cover up my bald spots today?

Although my mother was also suffering through the trauma of hair loss—and I'm assuming that sharing our fears would have helped me feel better—she never spoke to me about it. It was an unwritten rule in our home that we didn't talk about this kind of thing. We just didn't deal with problems at all. Consequently, I was very much alone in my struggle. Some of my girlfriends were pretty supportive, but the boys could be just plain mean. And, in their ignorance, adults were often cruel, too.

As my hair loss progressed, my teachers gave me permission to wear scarves and hats in class, even though they weren't generally allowed. But I remember one day when I had to deliver some papers to a teacher who didn't know me. I walked into the room, and the teacher stopped his class and turned around to look at me. Everyone else turned to look, too.

"Take that stupid scarf off your head," he said.

I was so mortified that I just ran out of his class, out of the school, and down the few blocks to my home. I couldn't stop crying. My parents went to school the next day to explain things to the teachers, but it seemed like the end of the world to me at the time.

By the mid-'60s, when I was in my twenties, hairpieces became popular, and that made my life much easier. Lots of my friends were experimenting with little hairpieces, or falls or wigs, and I could fit right in. I would attach a fall to my hair near the middle of my head and comb the front of my own hair back over it. It looked pretty natural. I had begun my career as a flight attendant by then, and fixing my hair with falls every morning really worked well for me.

Eventually, though, I didn't have enough hair left to attach any hairpieces. I started wearing my hair straight back into a bun then. But every time the wind blew, my bald spots would show. I was in my mid-twenties, and starting to feel hopeless.

Then one day, I saw a commercial on TV about hairpieces. In this commercial, a man jumped into a swimming pool, swam across the pool, popped up at the other end, and shook his head to get the water out of his hair. It was a hairpiece, but it didn't budge. I immediately called the phone number I saw on the screen. And based on about thirty seconds worth of information, I signed up to have a hairpiece surgically attached to my head. That's how desperate I was. I had sutures sewn around the circumference of my head, and a wig sewn to these sutures.

Not only did this give me the worst headaches I'd had in my life, but the sutures never healed. For an entire year and a half, I had open, oozing sores where each suture penetrated my scalp. And since the hairpiece was not removable, it eventually became filled with bacteria, perspiration, and oils. It was an awful, awful experience.

To top it off, I put a chemical color on the hairpiece. The hair color entered my system through the sores and made me so sick, I ended up in the hospital.

As sick as I was, and as much as I hated that hairpiece, it was my security blanket for eighteen months. When the hairpiece and sutures were removed in the hospital, I discovered I had become completely bald, and sank into a terrible depression. I had no idea where to turn. It was probably the worst feeling I've ever had in my life.

I refused to look at my head when I got out of the hospital. And actually, I hadn't really looked at myself for years before that hairpiece was sewn to my scalp. I had established elaborate procedures to avoid mirrors when I wasn't wearing a hairpiece. When I'd go into the bathroom to get ready to shower, I would make sure the vanity mirror was facing the wall. After I showered, I'd put on my hairpiece before I looked in the mirror to start my makeup. So I was in denial for a very long time.

When I left the hospital and my head healed, I began to wear wigs full-time. I carried on with my life as best as I could. But I was still carrying around a sense of embarrassment and shame about my hair loss. It was difficult for me to get close to people because I absolutely refused to talk about the alopecia. I figured it was my business and no one else's. But when you build a wall around one part of yourself, you tend to build it around your entire self.

Then, when I was about thirty, a miracle happened. It turned out that a neighbor of mine also had alopecia areata, and she had established an organization called the Alopecia Areata Foundation. She and I started sharing our hair loss stories. It was the very first time I'd ever spoken to another person about it. It felt so freeing to talk about it. When I realized all the years I spent in hiding, it seemed so sad. But once I started talking, I just felt this tremendous sense of freedom, freedom I've carried with me ever since.

My neighbor was so open and so accepting. For her, alopecia was part of who she was. And the more time I spent with her, the more comfortable I became with myself. After a while, I felt that I didn't have to hide my hair loss, and I didn't have to let it define me, either.

Before long, I started designing wigs in addition to continuing my work as a flight attendant. I did it part-time for a while, and do it full-time now. Then in 1997, a friend gave me a present that pointed me in a new direction. My best friend, Kathy, had always been so supportive of me. But I had never really understood how much one friend could do for another until Kathy gave me a most special present.

"This is the one thing you can't do for yourself," she said one day. And she handed me a thick plait of her own hair. She had grown it out and had it cut off just for me. I was so moved, and just about speechless at her generosity.

And then she said, "Wouldn't it be wonderful if lots of people could donate hair and you could make real-hair wigs for children? Wouldn't it be great if those kids didn't have to go through the trauma you went through?"

And based on that idea, Locks of Love was born. Locks of Love is a nonprofit organization that provides human-hair wigs for needy children under age eighteen. Some of the children we help have lost their hair through alopecia; others are burn victims or chemotherapy patients.

Since it takes about twelve donated ponytails to make one wig, I thought it would be great if we could provide two wigs a year to children. But we've had such a tremendous response that we've been able to provide forty-five wigs in the past eighteen months. About 80 percent of our donated hair comes from children—children who can imagine the pain of another child and are ready and willing to help.

I don't run Locks of Love on a day-to-day basis any more, but I am a volunteer, and I travel around the country to meet the children who are in need of wigs. I make molds of their heads, and design wigs to fit those molds.

When I first meet a child, they are always embarrassed and nervous. We sit and talk for a few minutes and they are usually squirming. And then I say, "OK, let me show you how this works."

And then off comes my own wig and—boom—they suddenly know I'm just like them. That's when their excitement really begins, and we're just off and running.

I absolutely love being with these kids. It is the most amazing feeling for me to bring them their finished wigs and watch as they put them on. When they look at themselves in the mirror with their new hair, you can actually see the sparkle return to their eyes. You can see their posture change. You can just feel their happiness and self-esteem all rushing back at once. I can't imagine a more wonderful feeling than sharing that moment.

And for me, it is such a healing experience. No matter how well adjusted I appear to be—and I know I look outwardly like a well-adjusted, successful woman—I am always going to carry a piece of this pain around inside of me. It's always going to hurt. So for me, each time I can give a child his or her happiness back, it's just a little bit more healing for me.

You may want to donate your hair for a child under eighteen with medical hair loss. Contact: Locks of Love, 2400 East Las Olas Boulevard, Suite 399, Ft. Lauderdale, Florida 33301. Tel: 888-896-1588. Fax: 954-523-8634. Web site: **www.locksoflove.org.**

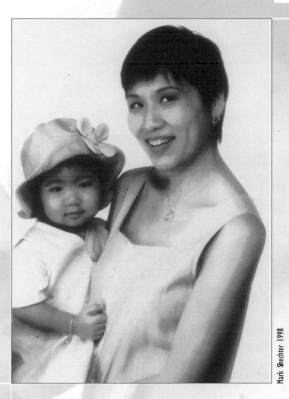

CHAPTER 30

Mark Shechter 1998

Dreams and Dragonflies

ADELIA DUNG

MY DAUGHTER, ALANA, WAS THE HAPPIEST OF CHILDREN. She was a warm, loving, funny, and friendly infant and toddler. Together with her older brother, Spencer, Alana brought happiness into our lives every day.

Alana was not a child destined to bring joy to her family alone. During her very short lifetime, Alana brought joy and a sense of purpose to tens of thousands of people. She became not only our little girl, but Hawaii's little girl. And even today, having left this earth, Alana continues to bring hope to people all over the world. ———————————————————————

Alana was just a year old in 1996, and my son, Spencer, was six. So when my husband, Steve, and I first realized Alana had a stomachache, we didn't worry too much at first. We had been through stomachaches with Spencer—all kids got them. But when her pain and fever persisted through several types of treatment, the doctors decided to do a bone marrow aspiration. What they found was that 70 percent of Alana's bone marrow was made up of leukemia cells.

Leukemia is a cancer of the bone marrow, and Alana had a rare type that was difficult to treat. We were told it was aggressive, and a bone marrow transplant was her only hope of survival.

It's hard to imagine any nightmare worse than having a child diagnosed with cancer. But unlike some families, we had no time to deal with our shock or fears or emotional pain. We knew Alana's only real chance for survival was finding a bone marrow donor. So we immediately focused on that task.

A bone marrow transplant isn't like any other kind of transplant. Bone marrow is donated by a living person, and the donor regenerates the marrow they give within a few weeks. The problem was finding someone whose marrow type exactly matched Alana's. If it weren't an exact match, her body would reject the donated marrow.

Bone marrow type is genetic, but neither Spencer nor any other family members was a perfect match. We searched the data banks of the national bone marrow registry. But even with 2.4 million volunteers, no one was a perfect match for Alana.

The only thing we could do to try to save our daughter was appeal to the public for help. We started out by working with Hawaii's donor registry to plan a bone marrow registration drive. At the drive, people would take a blood test to see whether or not they were a match for Alana. If they were a perfect match, their donation would involve a very simple surgical procedure, and they would leave the hospital the next day.

We chose a theme for our drive: "Expect a Miracle"—and we did. Miracles were all around. Not the ultimate one we'd hoped and prayed for for our Alana, but other miracles for us and for many, many people.

I will never forget what happened at our first drive. The media publicized Alana's story, and 1,000 people came out to help us that day—some of whom had to wait in line for as long as three hours. No one ever complained. Everyone waited. It was absolutely, overwhelmingly heartwarming to know that these people—these strangers—had come forward to try to save my daughter's life.

All together, we held twenty-two registry drives to try to find a match for Alana. Her story spread through the islands quickly, and people responded in ways I had never imagined.

I heard about a Honolulu taxi driver who offered free rides to people who would agree to join the registry. Imagine—he took time and money out of his pocket to get names onto the registry! One of his customers turned out to be the project chair of the San Diego chapter of the Leukemia Society of America Foundation. She was amazed to find a taxi driver who cared so deeply about bone marrow donor registration—a cause she was dedicated to. For a while, she said, it seemed like whenever she came to Honolulu, she got updated on Alana's status and the registry effort from whatever taxi she climbed into at the airport.

Our friends and relatives held drives on the mainland. Friends of my father's even went to the villages in China, where my husband's and my family originated, to test people. One of our cousins even saw Alana's picture in Italy.

During the period of one and a half months, when we held our drives, we received hundreds of letters from people telling us what Alana's struggle meant to them. One of the most remarkable was from a woman who rushed up to my husband at our last drive and pressed a small, stuffed bear into his arms. In a note, pinned to the bear's paw, she told us she was a parolee from prison.

"It doesn't seem fair," she wrote. "I messed up—made terrible mistakes—but here I am today, still alive, a free person, out of prison, with another chance to make something out of my life. But your daughter, who is completely innocent and good, is suffering terribly and may not have another chance. It doesn't seem fair." She told us Alana's cause had been adopted by prisoners throughout the state. They prayed for her every day.

I'll never forget that little note. It shows so clearly the way Alana's struggle affected so many people—even people who were themselves struggling and suffering to get through their days. Alana inspired people and brought them together in a miraculous way. She showed people that everyone has something wonderful to give. She inspired people to reach beyond what they are used to doing.

More than 30,000 people joined the bone marrow registry in hopes of saving Alana's life. That's an incredible number. It makes ours one of the ten largest bone marrow donor programs in the country.

Finally the good news came. We found a match for Alana from the Tzu Chi Foundation Registry in Taiwan. Grateful to have a donor, we turned to the Fred Hutchinson Cancer Research Center in Seattle. They agreed to do Alana's transplant.

A few weeks after Alana's second birthday, our whole family, including Alana's baby-sitter, went to Seattle. We settled into a condominium across the street from the hospital. It would be our home for six months.

Alana's transplant went well. There were some bumps along the road, but they were mostly predictable. The doctors and nurses quickly became her friends—and ours.

We made a conscious decision during that time to never treat Alana like a sick child. We never allowed anyone to cry in front of her. It was very important to me that Alana not be sad. We wanted her to be a happy, normal child as much as possible. And she was. Of course, as her vocabulary grew, she used words that other children didn't know, such as "blood drive" and "syringe." But to Alana, those words were normal. She didn't think of those words, or the hospital, as bad. And that really made it easier for all of us.

We did lose Alana in the end, but we had her with us for an entire extra year—and it was a wonderful year—simply because a stranger was willing to give her the ultimate gift of another chance at life.

When we finally lost Alana, there were moments I felt like I had lost everything that had ever meant anything to me. Every hope and every dream I ever had was crushed. I couldn't imagine the world would still turn, days would go by, clocks would tick, and appointments would be scheduled and kept. I couldn't believe my heart would keep on beating—that my breaths would keep coming, again and again and again. I felt like everything would have to stop.

Someone said something to me the day Alana died that I will never forget it: "If God had given you the choice of having her for just three years or not at all, which would you choose?"

That helped me put things in perspective. I chose to put my own pain aside and focus on my husband and son. And I promised myself I would continue to be an advocate for sick children.

I called Spencer's chaplain at school, a reverend named Lauren. She and Spencer had become very close before Alana's death, and I knew she could help him through this difficult time. In fact, the very first day he went back to school, Lauren read the children a little book that has become a central part of our lives.

It's called *Water Bugs and Dragonflies* by Doris Stickney. It tells the story of a group of water bugs who notice that every now and then, one of their members leaves and doesn't return. As the story unfolds, you see that the water bug has changed into a dragonfly. This dragonfly—beautiful and free as it soars and swoops in its new body—is happy, but it cannot communicate with its old friends. It has to wait until they become dragonflies, too.

Our whole family loved this story so much that we took the dragonfly on as our symbol for Alana. When she was alive, she used to hand out little angel lapel pins. She gave every person who cared for her an angel. Now we all wear a dragonfly. It reminds us that death is not an end, but a beginning.

Alana's illness exposed us to a world we hadn't known existed. So our great love now is to do advocacy with families, to help where we can. We've been there, we've seen the need, and now it's our job to fulfill that need. That's our philosophy of life, and it's really that simple. Every day we're learning something new. And every day, it's our job to do something with that newfound knowledge.

In addition to focusing on our family, we established the Alana Dung Research Foundation to support research directed at improving the quality of life for sick children, improving treatment, and preventing disease. Our first local grant, a $10,000 grant to the Hawaii Cord Blood Bank, is being used for genetic research. We call the Foundation newsletter "The Dragonfly."

We've also been working with the Hawaii Cord Blood Bank to establish a registry for umbilical cord blood, the latest weapon in the fight against leukemia and other similar diseases. On October 23, 1998—almost one year after Alana's death—we held a big fund-raiser in conjunction with the Blood Bank. The fund-raiser was called "Dreams and Dragonflies."

Alana gave us the gift of learning how to put things in perspective, how to focus on the simple things that most of us barely notice. She would thank the nurse for checking her blood pressure and showed her appreciation when assistance was given to her. Even in her pain, she would marvel at watching the ducks in the park, the boats on the lake, and the birds outside her hospital room.

Now we cherish those days, those memories, and those pictures of her precious angelic smile and sparkling dark, doe-like eyes. Yes, they might have been taken in a hospital, with Alana hooked up to tubes and machines, but that doesn't detract from the value of the time we shared or our deep love and happiness at being together.

Alana has left us and gone on to her new life, but the legacy she left behind is very much alive right here. Among the 30,000 people who came forward to try to save Alana's life, fifty of them have gone on to become a perfect match for other patients in less than three years. Fifty families who were waiting and waiting have felt the joy of having a second chance at life. That's how Alana's suffering has borne fruit in the world.

To those fifty families—and to the hundreds and hundreds of families "Alana's volunteers" will surely touch over the coming years—the legacy of our little girl is alive and well. She lived only three short years. But, using her wings now, she will continue to bring the gift of life to special people throughout the world. With each new day, I am able to appreciate the wonderful gift that Alana's time with us really was.

A friend recently described my experiences of the past few years as living through a kind of hell. But nothing could be farther from the truth. Yes, having to give up a child is pure, searing, indescribable pain that will never go away. But in all honesty, I feel I have been granted a glimpse of heaven, not hell. Thanks to Alana, strangers have reached out to one another, willingly given of their time, energy, and imagination. Inspired by Alana, people from all walks of life reaffirm the best part of their humanity. That's what heaven is: giving of ourselves selflessly and lovingly to anyone in need.

What greater legacy could any of us ever hope to leave?

Learn more about bone marrow donation and/or ways you can help save lives by contacting: The Alana Dung Research Foundation, 1210 Auahi Street, Suite 201, Honolulu, Hawaii 96814. Tel: 808-591-8293. Fax: 808-593-2921. E-mail: adelia@aloha.net.

MISFORTUNE, ILLNESS, PERSONAL TRIAL, AND CATASTROPHE—whatever we label it—is such an egocentric thing. "Woe is me!" is an appropriate response. But this book reminds us that it is only a point of departure. Here, in these pages, we are taught what the next step is, and the next, and the next. This is a book about healing through fixing the world, making it a more decent and caring place. The profiles in this book are, indeed, inspirational, and we need inspiration, all of us. We need it to enliven us (and if we are despairing, to revivify us, move us beyond ourselves to doing for others).

When the time comes (which is now, always now) to comfort a human being in a hospice or hospital, a school or at home, these are the people who will show us how to touch or embrace a person. When a cold diagnosis is rendered and the patient is lost in profound distress and confusion, these people—the Caridad Asensios, the Bea Salazars, the Sue Turks, and Barbara Pittmans—will teach us the appropriate words and silences that are so desperately needed. What better teachers could we ask for? We are fortunate that they are with us, that we can meet them or read about them, and learn what is good, and just, and right in life. Herein lies the story—many stories—of greatness, of humanity at its best. Most of all, it is a guide to action. We should all be grateful for this book. We are much the better for it.

Now we must fulfill the words and dreams of the people who tell us their stories. We must go out into the world and make things happen, good things, uplifting things. And yes, we must risk admitting to ourselves that we will be an inspiration to others to do the same. I, for one, am most grateful. I won't thank Ms. Waldman. She would be embarrassed. She is just doing what she thinks she should be doing. Let's leave it at this: I will spare her the unwanted attention and simply say, I am just grateful in general.

Danny Siegel is the author of more that twenty-four books on topics such as mitzvah heroes and practical and personalized giving. He is the founder of the Ziv Tzedakah Fund, a nonprofit mitzvah organization that has distributed over 3 million dollars to worthy individuals and projects. Web site: **www.ziv.org.**

> *"Do you see O my brothers and sisters?*
> *It is not chaos or death—it is form, union,*
> *plan—it is eternal life—it is Happiness."*

> —WALT WHITMAN, "SONG OF MYSELF"

THE MOST REVOLUTIONARY ACT ANYONE CAN COMMIT IS TO BE HAPPY. I refer not to a moment of joy during one of life's peak experiences, but to a basic pattern of enduring happiness. It takes no greater effort to be happy every day than to be miserable.

Each of us chooses the background hues of his or her own portrait. Unfortunately, a paradigm of suffering and unhappiness seems to have dominated human awareness during the past 5,000 years, with a basic, underlying feeling that life is a struggle. However, this could change, and happiness could become the foundation from which life is launched. We can *choose* a paradigm of happiness in which all our thoughts, feelings, and actions are infused with joy.

It takes great effort to reject joy and beauty; it is not a passive act. With all the potential for happiness in this world, it is astounding that people are so bored and lonely. I do not intend to trivialize sadness or anxiety but simply to say that we choose these ways of life. People who feel sad tend to blame external events over which they have no control. This is irresponsible. Such individuals become accomplices to the paradigm of pain when they sign out the "script" of a victim. Yes, the terrible things that happen are painful. Choosing to give up, however, is what makes these experiences continue to wound us.

Viktor E. Frankl, a survivor of the Nazi concentration camps who knows the importance of freedom of choice, wrote in *Man's Search for Meaning:* "We who lived in concentration camps can remember the men who walked through the huts comforting others, giving away their last piece of bread. They may have been few in number, but they offer sufficient proof that everything can be taken away from a man but one thing: the last of the human freedoms—to choose one's attitude in any given set of circumstances, to choose one's own way."

I am interested in happiness because I am a physician. Over the years, I have interviewed thousands of people extensively. Most say happiness is a rare commodity in their lives and can list the few specific times they were happy. People often decline to do things that would make them happy—a physician must completely ignore huge areas of a patient's life because the patient doesn't want to make lifestyle changes. With great sadness, we prescribe treatments that we know will only partially help.

Love is the most important ingredient in a healthy, happy life. The study of love is no longer the exclusive realm of the artist. Scientists now have conclusive evidence that it is the most important stress-reducing force known, just as loss or lack of love is the most potent disease-promoting force. These studies are explained in *Love, Medicine & Miracles* by Bernie Siegel, a surgeon at Yale. If love is the foundation for happiness, then fun, play, and laughter are the vehicles for its expression. The great physician Sir William Osler said that laughter is the "music of life." And one of humor's important psychological functions is to transform old habits into new perspectives and behaviors.

Unless individuals have given some form of service, I believe that it will be difficult for them to feel that life is ultimately fulfilling. John Donne wrote, "No man is an Island" to acknowledge that we all are connected in some way. Only by helping others can we discover deep interdependence. It is vital that service be performed out of thanks and the joy of giving, because service easily can rise to a debit/credit mentality. Service can take many forms: being a loving friend, helping a stranger in need, strengthening the community one lives in.

We must cast off fear and doubt, and learn to love and care for all people without waiting for others to take the first step.

I am suggesting that even though the world's pain hurts us, we must keep love and peace in our lives. We must take every opportunity to shout, "Whoopee!" Be an example of joy!

Patch Adams, M.D. is a physician, author, and the founder of Gesundheit! Institute. Web site: **www.patchadams.org.**

The people profiled in this book have compiled the following list of books that have been particularly influential in their lives:

Adams, Patch, M.D. *Gesundheit! Bringing Good Health to You, the Medical System, and Society Through Physician Service, Complementary Therapies, Humor, and Joy.* Pittsboro, North Carolina: Healing Arts, 1998.

Arnold, Johann Christoph. *Seeking Peace: Notes and Conversations along the Way.* Farmington, Pennsylvania: Plough Publishing House, 1998.

Ashe, Arthur, and Arnold Rampersad. *Days of Grace: A Memoir.* New York: Ballentine Books Inc., 1994.

Bonhoeffer, Dietrich. *The Cost of Discipleship.* New York: Simon & Schuster, 1995.

Brinker, Nancy. *The Race Is Run One Step at a Time.* Arlington, Texas: Summit Publishing Group, 1995.

Buscaglia, Leo. *Living, Loving, and Learning.* New York: Fawcett Books, 1990.

Caras, Roger. *A Perfect Harmony: The Intertwining Lives of Animals and Humans throughout History.* New York: Fireside, 1997.

de Caussade, Jean-Pierre, and John Beevers. *Abandonment to Divine Providence.* Chicago: Triumph Books, 1995.

Central Conference of American Rabbis. *Gates of Prayer.* New York: Central Conference of American Rabbis, 1975.

Community of Kindness: Reconnecting to Friends, Family, and the World Through the Power of Kindness. Berkeley, California: Conari Press, 1999.

Dosick, Wayne. *When Life Hurts: A Book of Hope.* San Francisco: HarperSanFrancisco, 1998.

Dyer, Wayne. *Real Magic: Creating Miracles in Everyday Life*. New York: HarperCollins, 1993.

Evans, Nicholas. *The Horse Whisperer.* New York: Bantam Books, 1996.

Forward, Susan, M.D. *Toxic Parents: Overcoming Their Hurtful Legacy and Reclaiming Your Life*. New York: Bantam Books, 1990.

Foundation for Inner Peace. *A Course in Miracles: Combined Volume*. New York: Viking Press, 1996.

Frank, Anne, and B. M. Mooyaart. *Anne Frank: The Diary of a Young Girl*. New York: Bantam Books, 1993.

Fuller, Millard. *The Theology of the Hammer.* Macon, Georgia: Smyth & Helwys Publishers, 1994.

Keene, Nancy. *Childhood Leukemia: A Guide for Families, Friends & Caregivers*. Cambridge, Massachusetts: O'Reilly & Associates, 1997.

Komp, Diane M., M.D. *A Window to Heaven: When Children See Life in Death*. Grand Rapids, Michigan: Zondervan Publishing House, 1992.

Kushner, Rabbi Harold. *When Bad Things Happen to Good People*. New York: Avon Books, 1992.

Lasher, Margot. *And the Animals Will Teach You: Discovering Ourselves through Our Relationship with Animals*. New York: Berkley Publishing Group, 1996.

Lee, Harper. *To Kill a Mockingbird*. Toronto, Ontario, Canada: McClelland & Stewart, 1969.

Leeland, Jeff. *One Small Sparrow: The Remarkable, Real-Life Drama of One Community's Compassionate Response to a Little Boy's Life*. Sisters, Oregon: Multnomah Publishers, Inc., 1995.

Lowry, Lois. *Number the Stars*. New York: Laurel-Leaf, 1998.

Lozoff, Bo. *We're All Doing Time: A Guide for Getting Free*. Durham, North Carolina: Human Kindness Foundation, 1985.

Lunden, Joan. *A Bend in the Road Is Not the End of the Road: 10 Positive Principles for Dealing With Change*. New York, New York: William Morrow & Company, 1998.

Medlock, Ann, and staff. *The Giraffe Heroes Program*. Seattle, Washington: The Giraffe Project, 1997.

Mitchell, W, with Brad Lemley. *It's not What Happens to You, It's What You Do about It*. Denver: Phoenix Press, 1997.

Moyer, Jeff. *We're People First: Songs for Inclusive Schools and Communities*. Cleveland: Music From the Heart, 1995.

Nicarthy, Ginny. *You Can Be Free: An Easy-to-Read Handbook for Abused Women*. Seattle, Washington: Seal Press Feminist Publications, 1997.

Random Acts of Kindness. Berkeley, California: Conari Press, 1993.

Rawls, Wilson. *Where the Red Fern Grows*. New York: Bantam Starfire, 1984.

Ryan, Mary Jane. *Attitudes of Gratitude: How to Give and Receive Joy Everyday of Your Life*. Berkeley, California: Conari Press, 1999.

de Saint-Exupéry, Antoine. *The Little Prince*. New York: Harcourt Brace, 1968.

Sams, Jamie, and Linda Childers. *Sacred Path Cards: The Discovery of Self through Native Teachings*. San Francisco: HarperSanFrancisco, 1990.

Schoen, Allen M. and Pam Proctor. *Love, Miracles, and Animal Healing: A Heartwarming Look at the Spiritual Bond between Animals and Humans*. New York: Fireside, 1996.

Siegel, Danny. *Healing: Readings and Meditations*. Pittsboro, North Carolina: The Town House Press, 1999.

Shapiro, Joseph P. *No Pity: People with Disabilities Forging a New Civil Rights Movement*. New York: Times Books, 1994.

Stickney, Doris. *Waterbugs and Dragonflies: Explaining Death to Young Children*. Cleveland, Ohio: Pilgrim Press, 1997.

Thomas, William H., M.D. *Learning from Hannah: Secrets for a Life Worth Living*. VanderWyk & Burnham, 1999.

Villa, Richard A. and Jacqueline Thousand. *Creating an Inclusive School*. Alexandria, Virginia: Association for Supervision and Curriculum Development, 1996.

Weiss, Lynn. *A.D.D. and Creativity*. Dallas: Taylor Publishing Company, 1997.

_____. *Give Your ADD Teen a Chance*. Dallas: Taylor Publishing Company, 1996.

To Steve—my soulmate—for your love and support.

To Melissa, Todd, and Michael—my precious cargo—for the lessons we learn together.

To Mother and Daddy and Mom and Dad—for giving me the tools to grow.

To Ellen, Tommy, Holly, Mike, Carol, Howard, Cherie, and Neal—for being all that great sisters and brothers are.

To Tootsie—my angel of humor and kindness—whom I think of daily.

To Dee—my spiritual sister—for all we share.

To Mary Jane Ryan—my extraordinary editor and friend—for your amazing skills and huge heart.

To Brenda and Nancy—for your tireless energy and belief that anything is possible.

To the entire group at Conari—for your genius, dedication, and enthusiasm.

To Jim Levine—my agent and advisor—for your expertise and vision.

To Karen Frost—my publicist—for your devotion to the project.

To Judy Williams—my transcriber—for your hard work and kindness.

To Fran, Jen, Marcy, and Mick—for your help with this project—for your friendship.

To Susan—my friend and talented photographer—for your understanding of the big picture.

To Janis—my friend and gifted writer—for saying "yes" and making this project a reality through your talent and compassionate soul.

To Patch Adams, Joan Lunden, and Danny Siegel—for your heartfelt messages.

To thirty wonderful people for sharing your message of truth and healing.

My deep felt thanks and love.

—J.W.

To Chip, Daniel, and Michael—for your love and encouragement. More than anything else, it is your very existence and your love that has revealed to me the miracle and beauty of God's creation.

To Mom, Dad, Nana, Papa, Janie, Louis, David, and Johnny—those here in body and those here only in spirit—for your continual love and guidance.

To Christine, Lynn N., Lynn W., "Maaarilyn," and Sally—for the depth of your love and friendship.

And to Jackie—my friend whose heart and soul heard the message and brought this project to life—for believing in me and leading me to these thirty beautiful teachers.

Thank you.
—J.L.D.

In addition to cofounding Dallas' Random Acts of Kindness™ Week, JACKIE WALDMAN has volunteered for the Multiple Sclerosis Society, the March of Dimes, the National Council of Jewish Women, and the Dallas Memorial Center for Holocaust Studies. A recipient of *Girls, Inc.*'s 1999 "She Knows Where She's Going" Award, Jackie is a member of the advisory board for Our Friend's Place, a safe haven for abused girls. She lives in Dallas, Texas, with her husband, three children, and two dogs.

> If you have ever faced a physical or emotional obstacle in your life, reached out to help others and learned that by helping others, you ultimately helped yourself, I want to hear from you. Contact me at my website at: www.couragetogive.com

JANIS LEIBS DWORKIS is a writer and editor who has produced more than 250 stories for, among others, *The Dallas Morning News, American Baby,* and *Spirit Magazine.* The editor of eight books, she lives in Dallas, Texas, with her husband and two children.

Conari Press, established in 1987, publishes books on topics
ranging from psychology, spirituality, and women's history to
sexuality, parenting, and personal growth. Our main goal is
to publish quality books that will make a difference
in people's lives—both how we feel about ourselves
and how we relate to one another.

Our readers are our most important resource,
and we value your input, suggestions, and ideas.
We'd love to hear from you—after all,
we are publishing books for you!

To request our latest book catalog,
or to be added to our mailing list,
please contact:

CONARI PRESS
2550 Ninth Street, Suite 101
Berkeley, California 94710-2551
800-685-9595 510-649-7175
fax: 510-649-7190
e-mail: conari@conari.com
www.conari.com